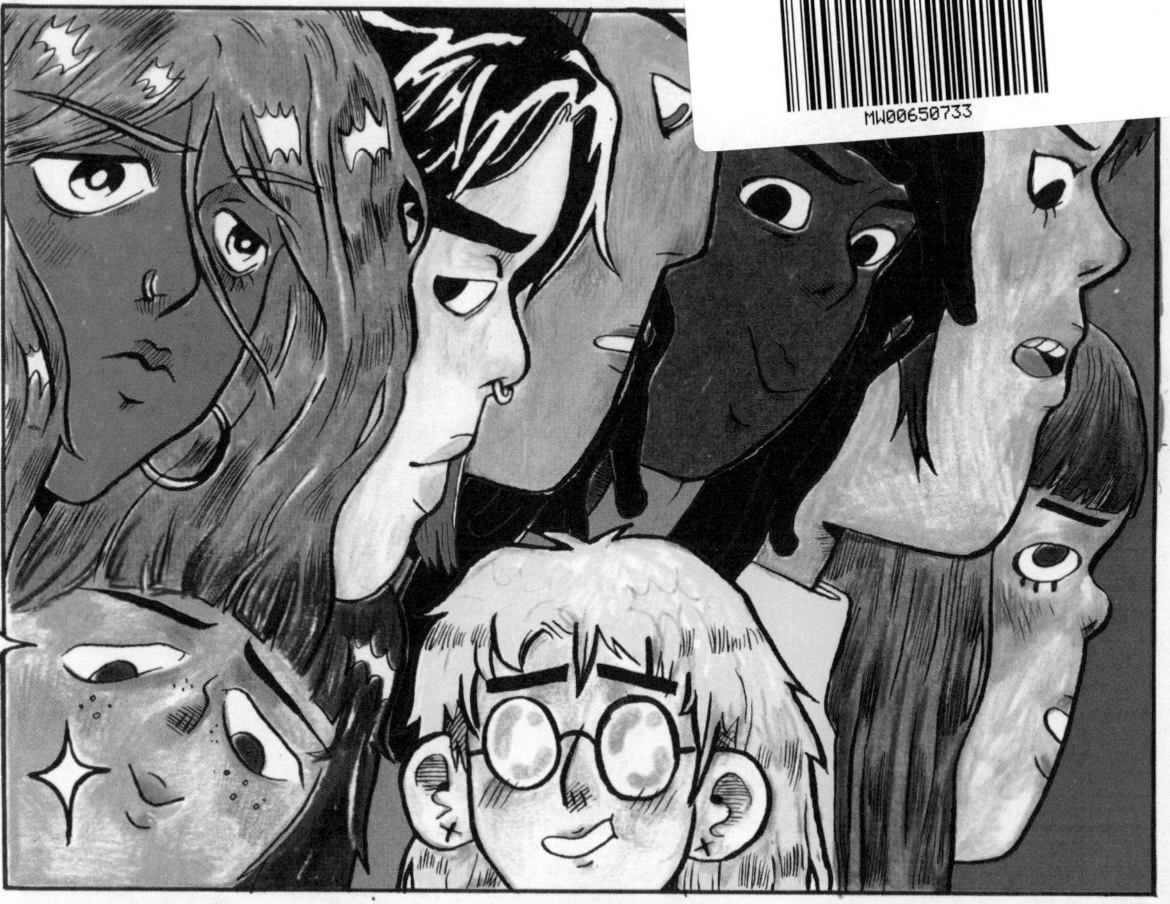

GIRL IN THE WORLD

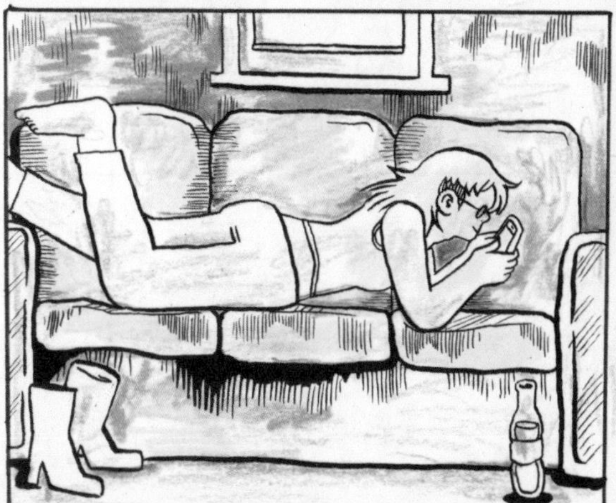

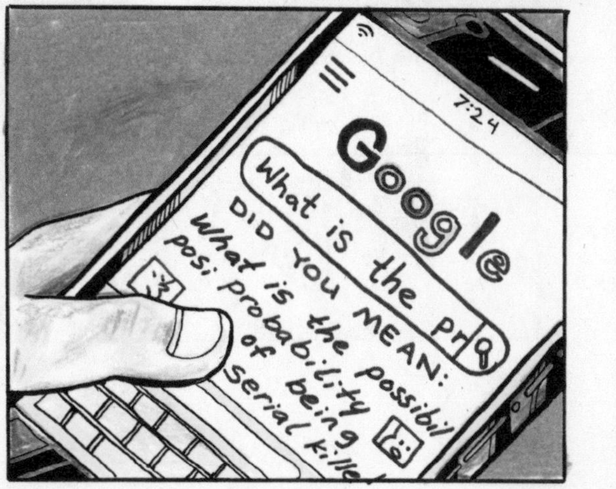
7:24
Google
What is the pr
DID YOU MEAN:
What is the possibil
posi probability
of being
serial killed

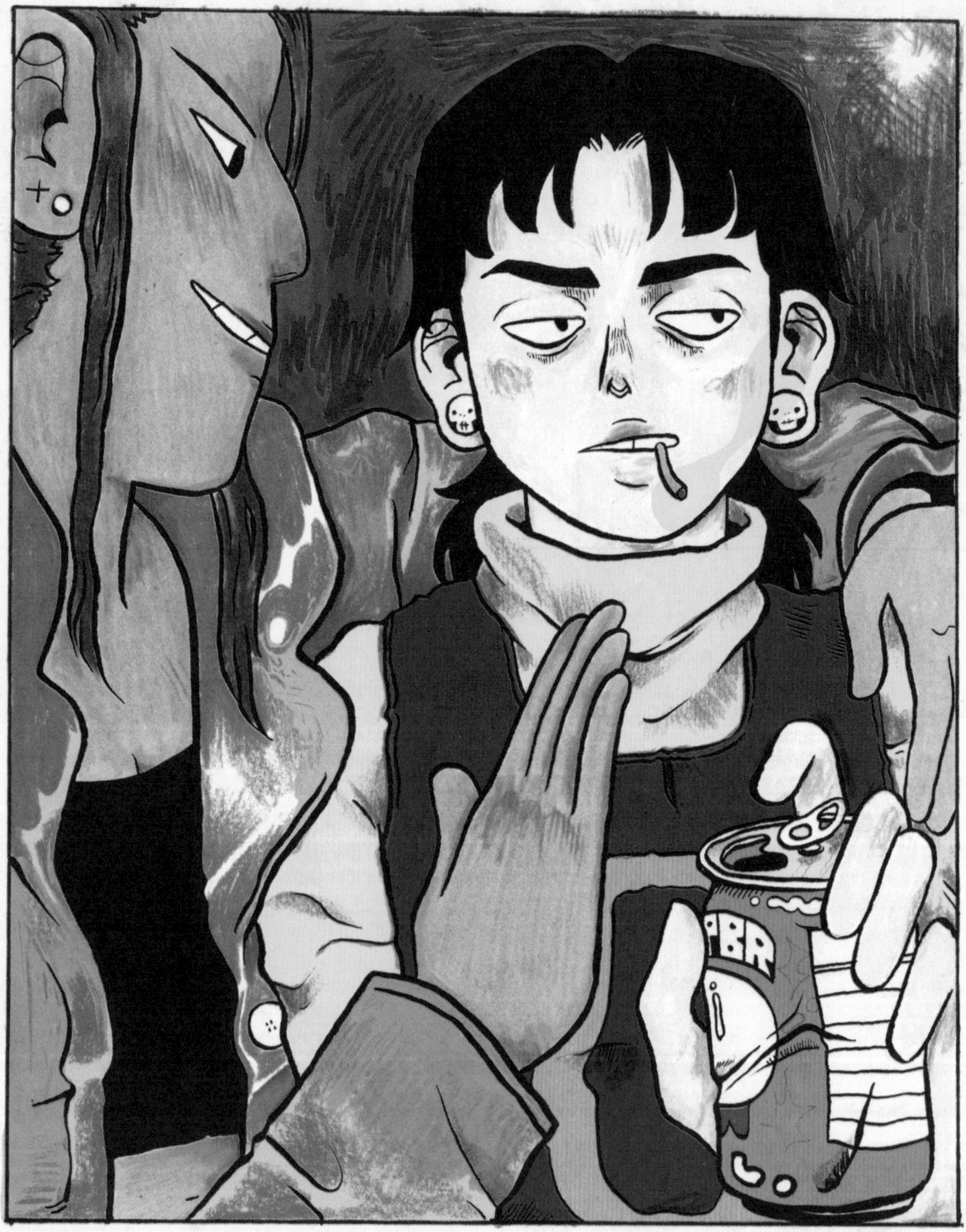
PBR

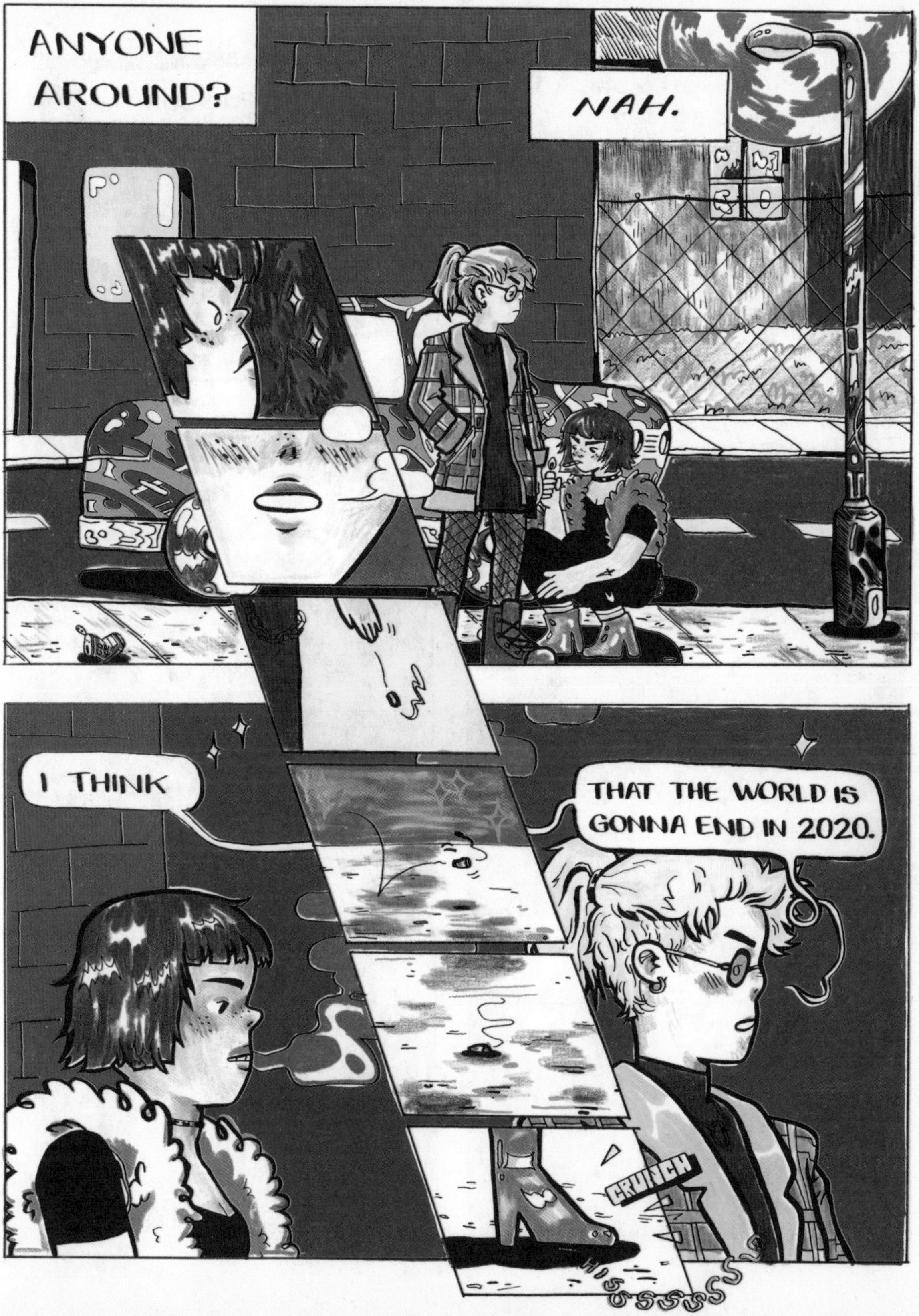
ANYONE AROUND?
NAH.
I THINK
THAT THE WORLD IS GONNA END IN 2020.
CRUNCH

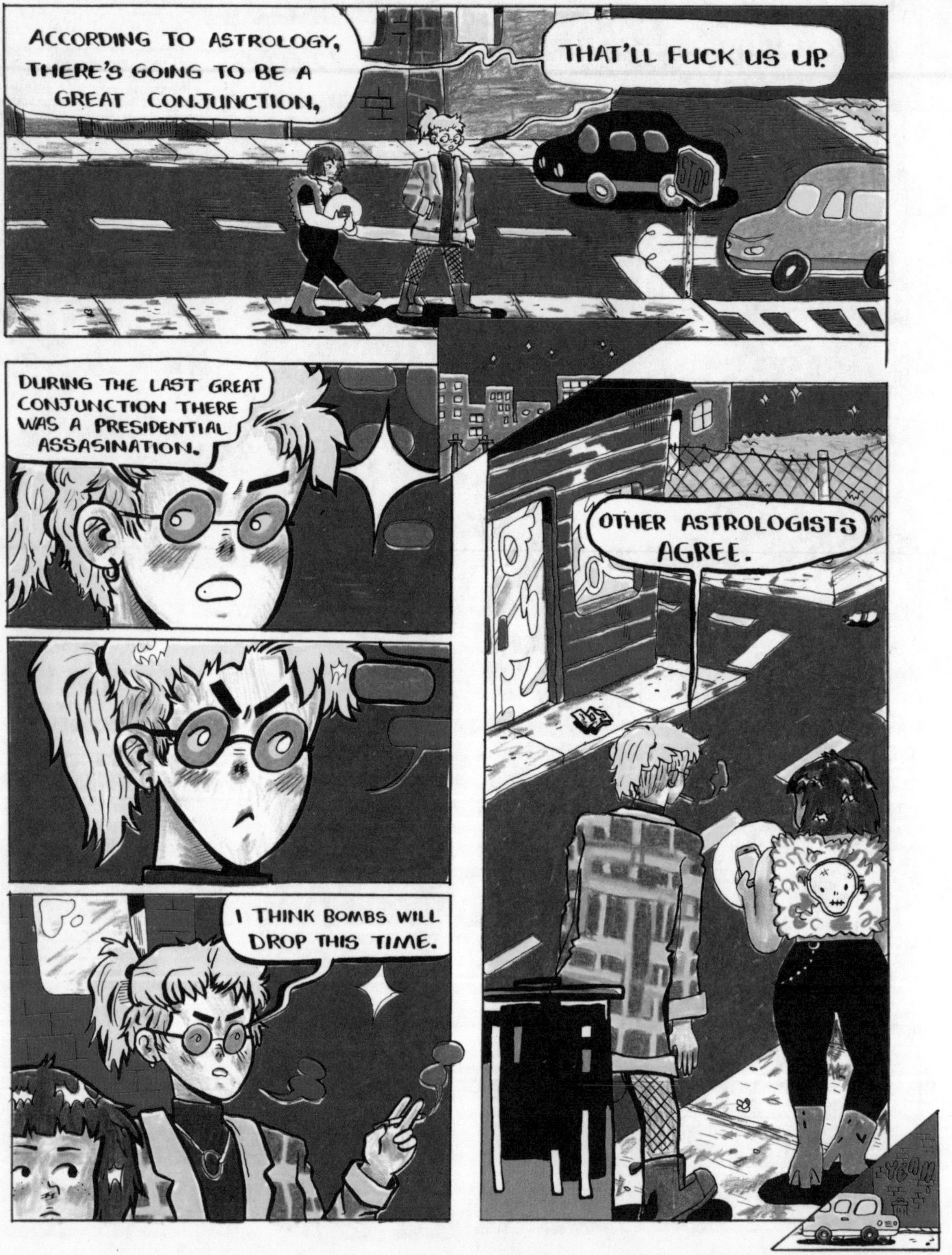

ACCORDING TO ASTROLOGY, THERE'S GOING TO BE A GREAT CONJUNCTION,
THAT'LL FUCK US UP.
STOP
DURING THE LAST GREAT CONJUNCTION THERE WAS A PRESIDENTIAL ASSASINATION.
OTHER ASTROLOGISTS AGREE.
I THINK BOMBS WILL DROP THIS TIME.

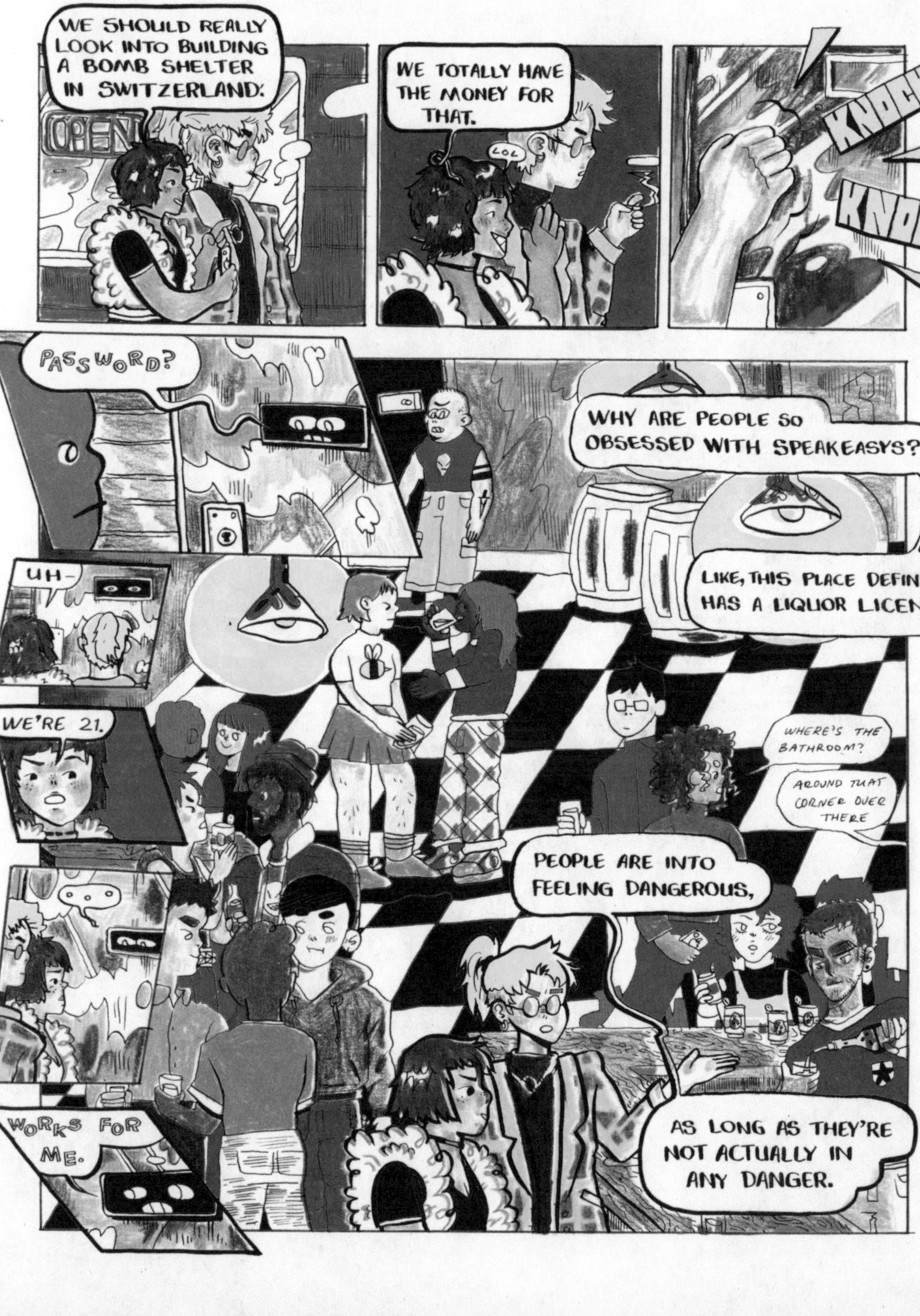
WE SHOULD REALLY LOOK INTO BUILDING A BOMB SHELTER IN SWITZERLAND.
OPEN
WE TOTALLY HAVE THE MONEY FOR THAT.
LOL
KNOCK
KNOCK
PASSWORD?
UH-
WE'RE 21.
...
WORKS FOR ME.
WHY ARE PEOPLE SO OBSESSED WITH SPEAKEASYS?
LIKE, THIS PLACE DEFINITELY HAS A LIQUOR LICENSE.
WHERE'S THE BATHROOM?
AROUND THAT CORNER OVER THERE
PEOPLE ARE INTO FEELING DANGEROUS,
AS LONG AS THEY'RE NOT ACTUALLY IN ANY DANGER.

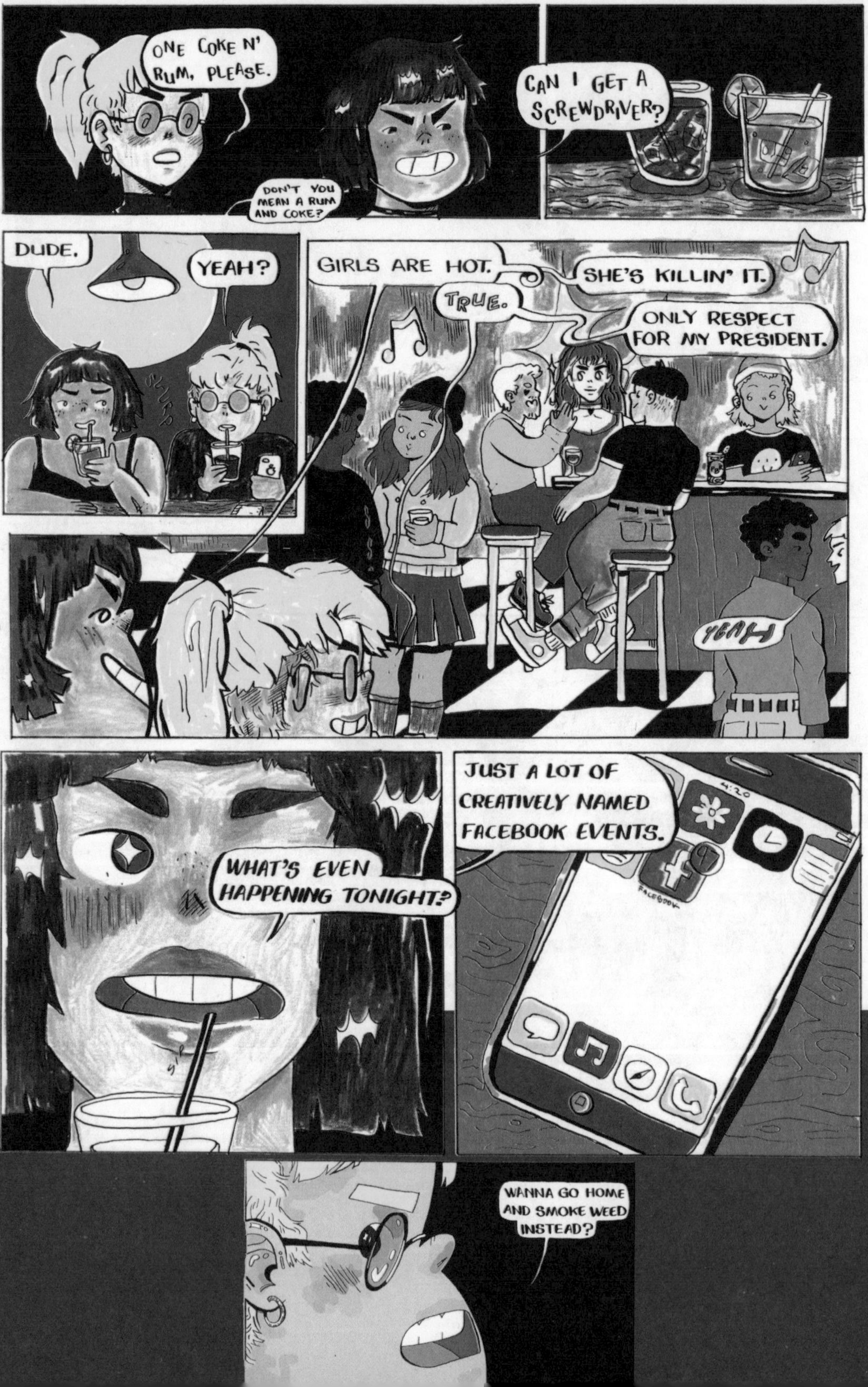
ONE COKE N' RUM, PLEASE.
DON'T YOU MEAN A RUM AND COKE?
CAN I GET A SCREWDRIVER?
DUDE.
YEAH?
GIRLS ARE HOT.
TRUE.
SHE'S KILLIN' IT.
ONLY RESPECT FOR MY PRESIDENT.
YEAH
WHAT'S EVEN HAPPENING TONIGHT?
JUST A LOT OF CREATIVELY NAMED FACEBOOK EVENTS.
4:20
FACEBOOK
WANNA GO HOME AND SMOKE WEED INSTEAD?

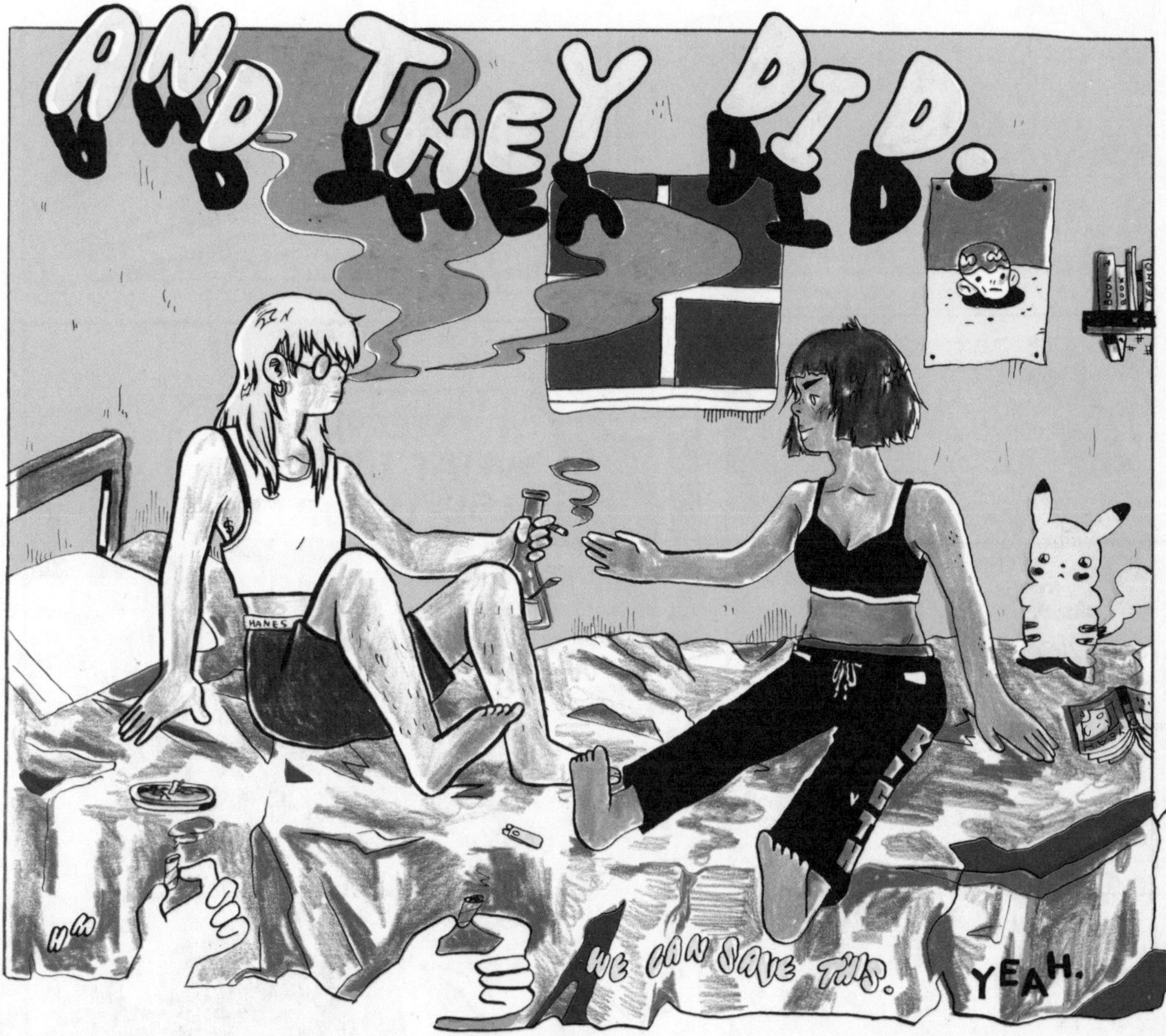
AND THEY DID.
HANES
HM
WE CAN SAVE THIS.
YEAH.

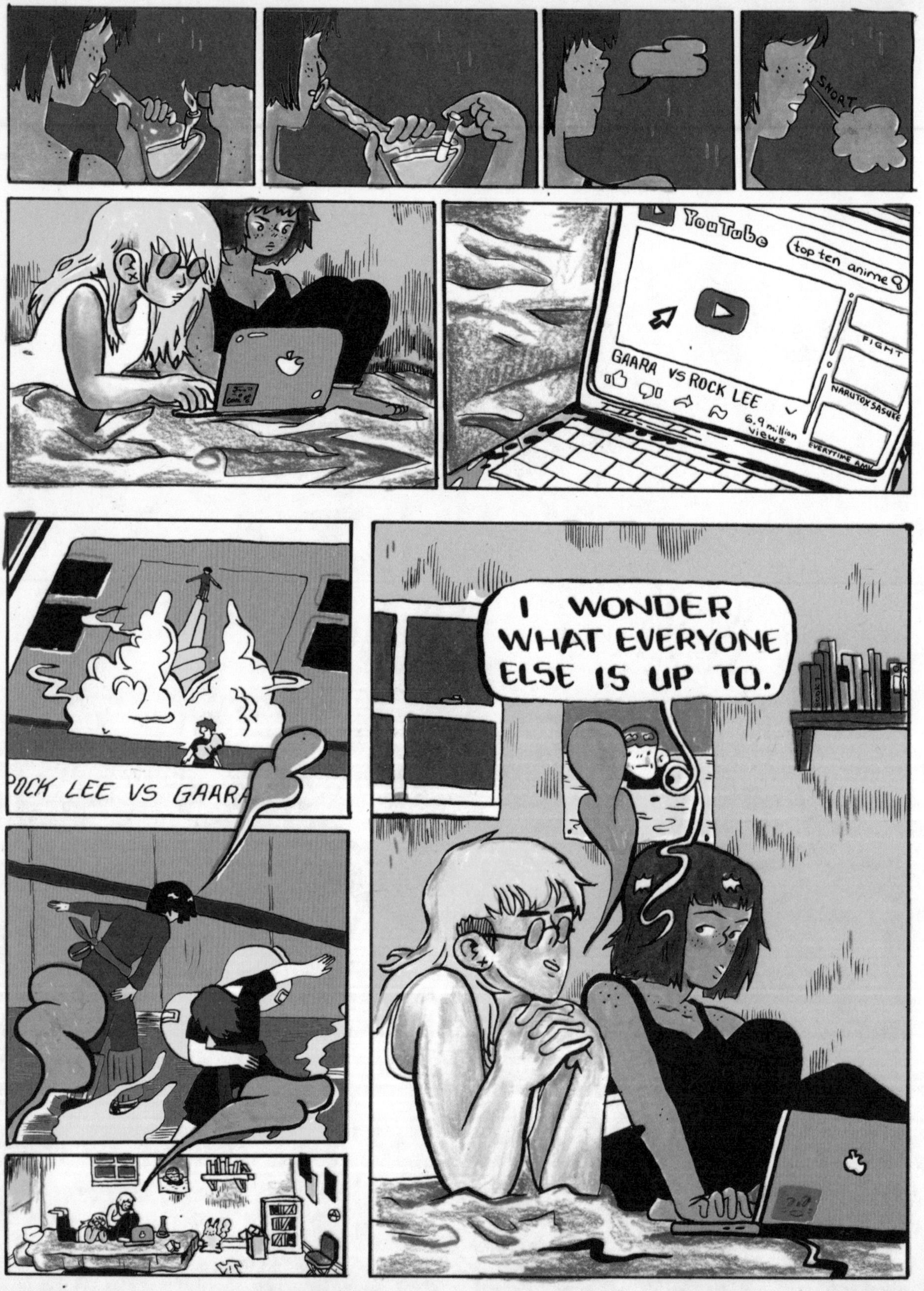
SNORT
YouTube
top ten anime
GAARA VS ROCK LEE
6.9 million views
FIGHT
NARUTOXSASUKE
EVERYTIME AMV
ROCK LEE VS GAARA
I WONDER WHAT EVERYONE ELSE IS UP TO.

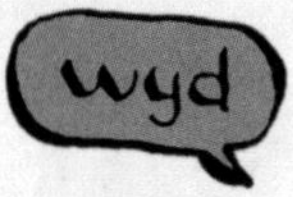
wyd

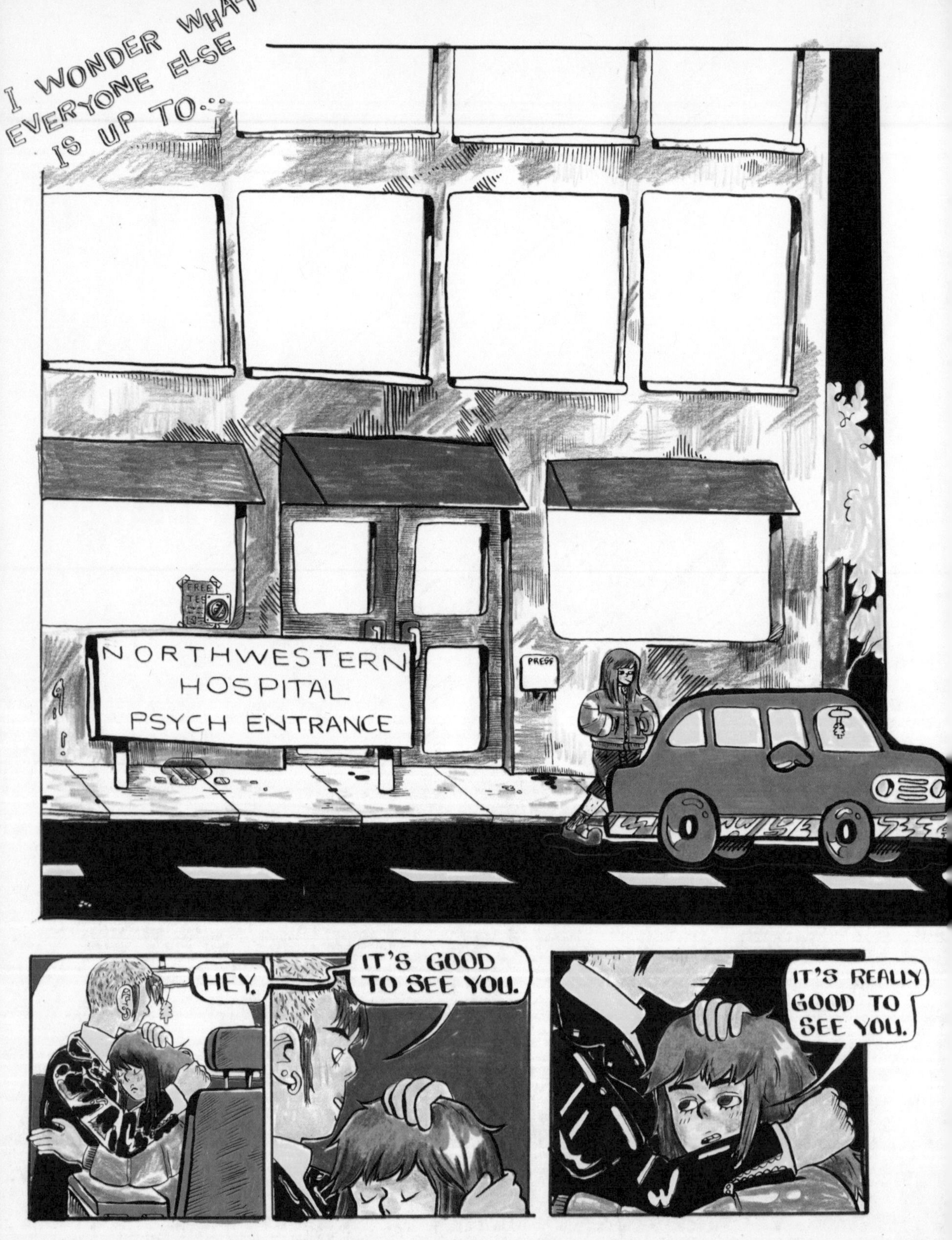
I WONDER WHAT EVERYONE ELSE IS UP TO...
NORTHWESTERN HOSPITAL PSYCH ENTRANCE
PRESS
HEY.
IT'S GOOD TO SEE YOU.
IT'S REALLY GOOD TO SEE YOU.

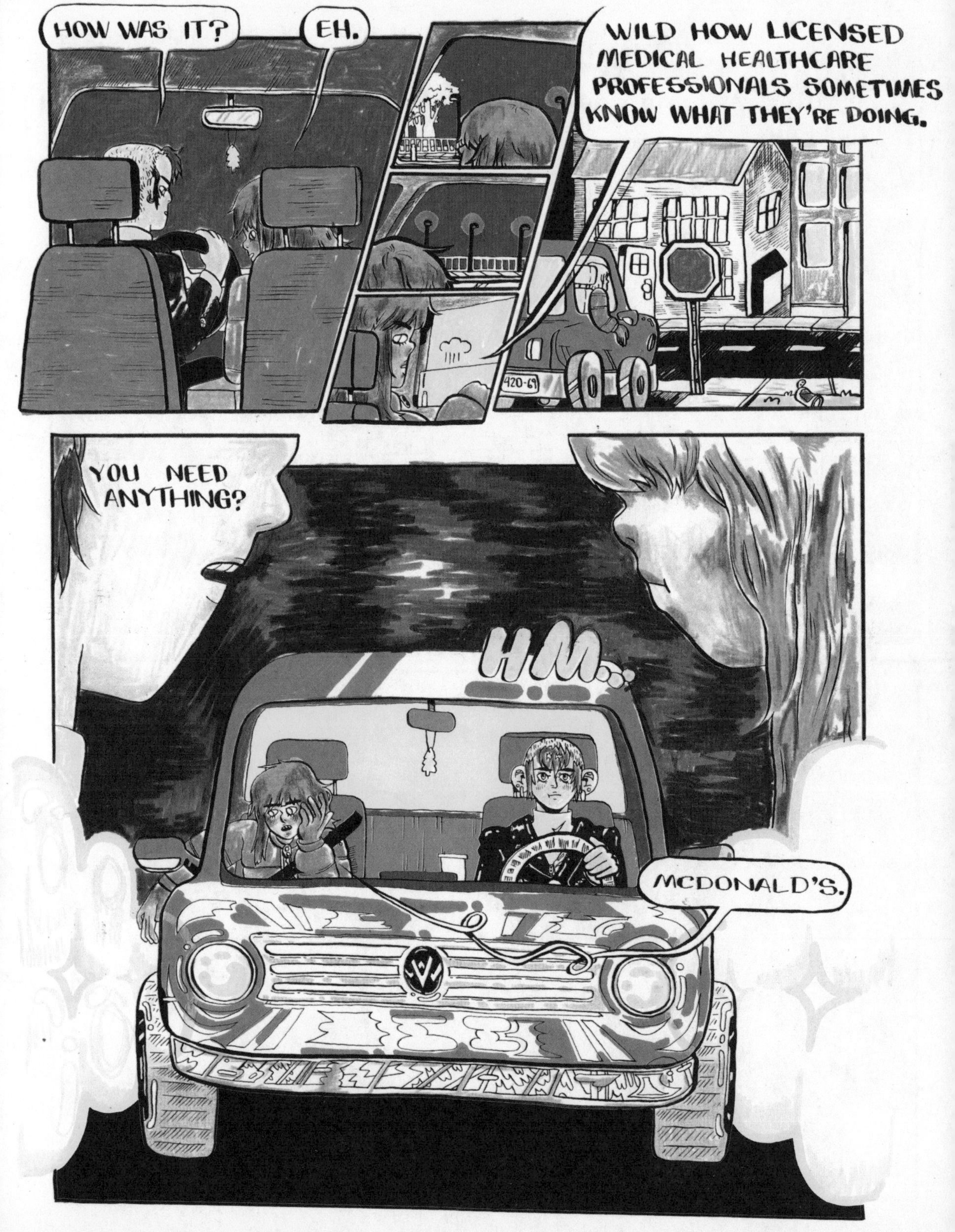
HOW WAS IT?
EH.
WILD HOW LICENSED MEDICAL HEALTHCARE PROFESSIONALS SOMETIMES KNOW WHAT THEY'RE DOING.
420-69
YOU NEED ANYTHING?
HM...
MCDONALD'S.

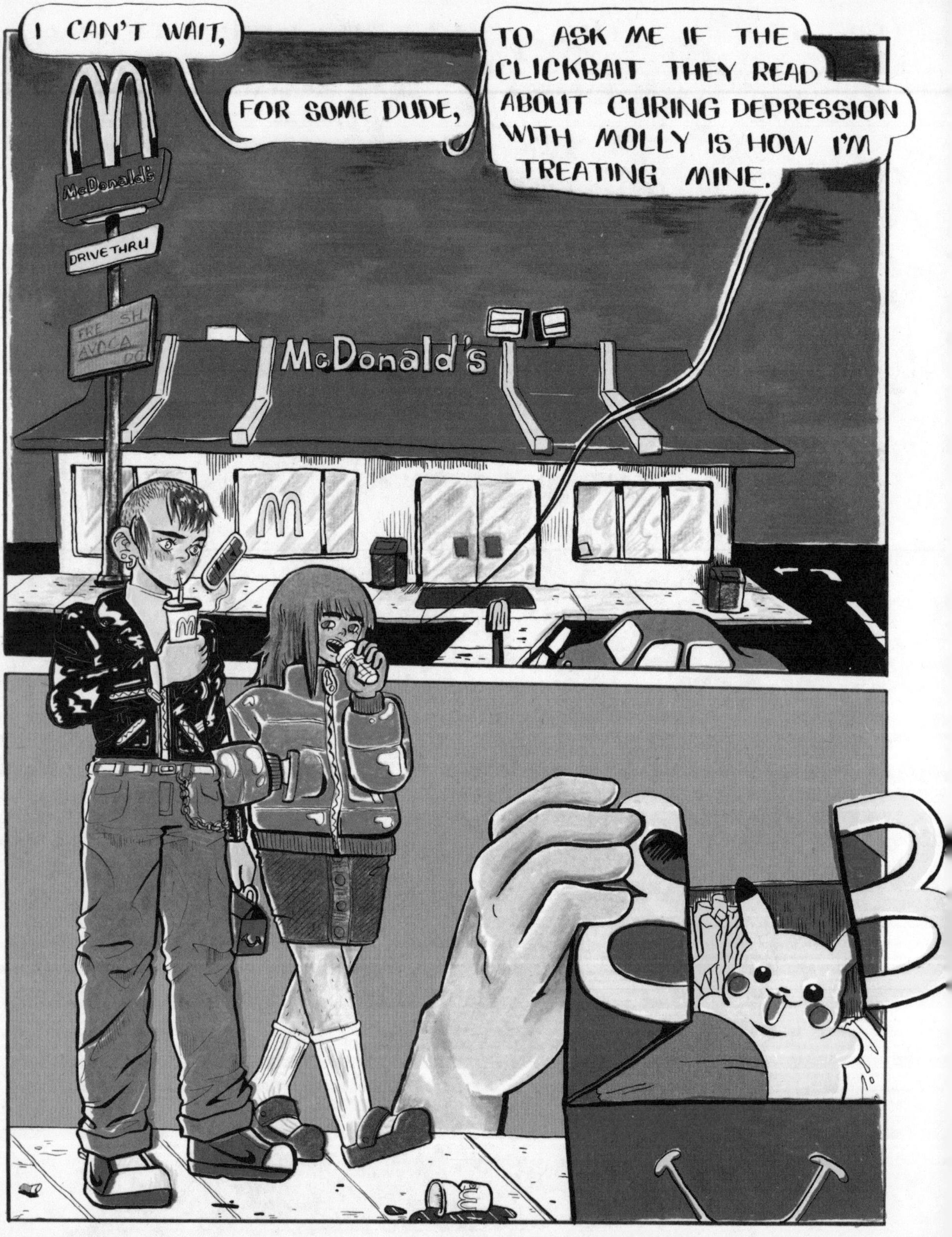
I CAN'T WAIT,
FOR SOME DUDE,
TO ASK ME IF THE CLICKBAIT THEY READ ABOUT CURING DEPRESSION WITH MOLLY IS HOW I'M TREATING MINE.
McDonald's
DRIVE THRU
McDonald's

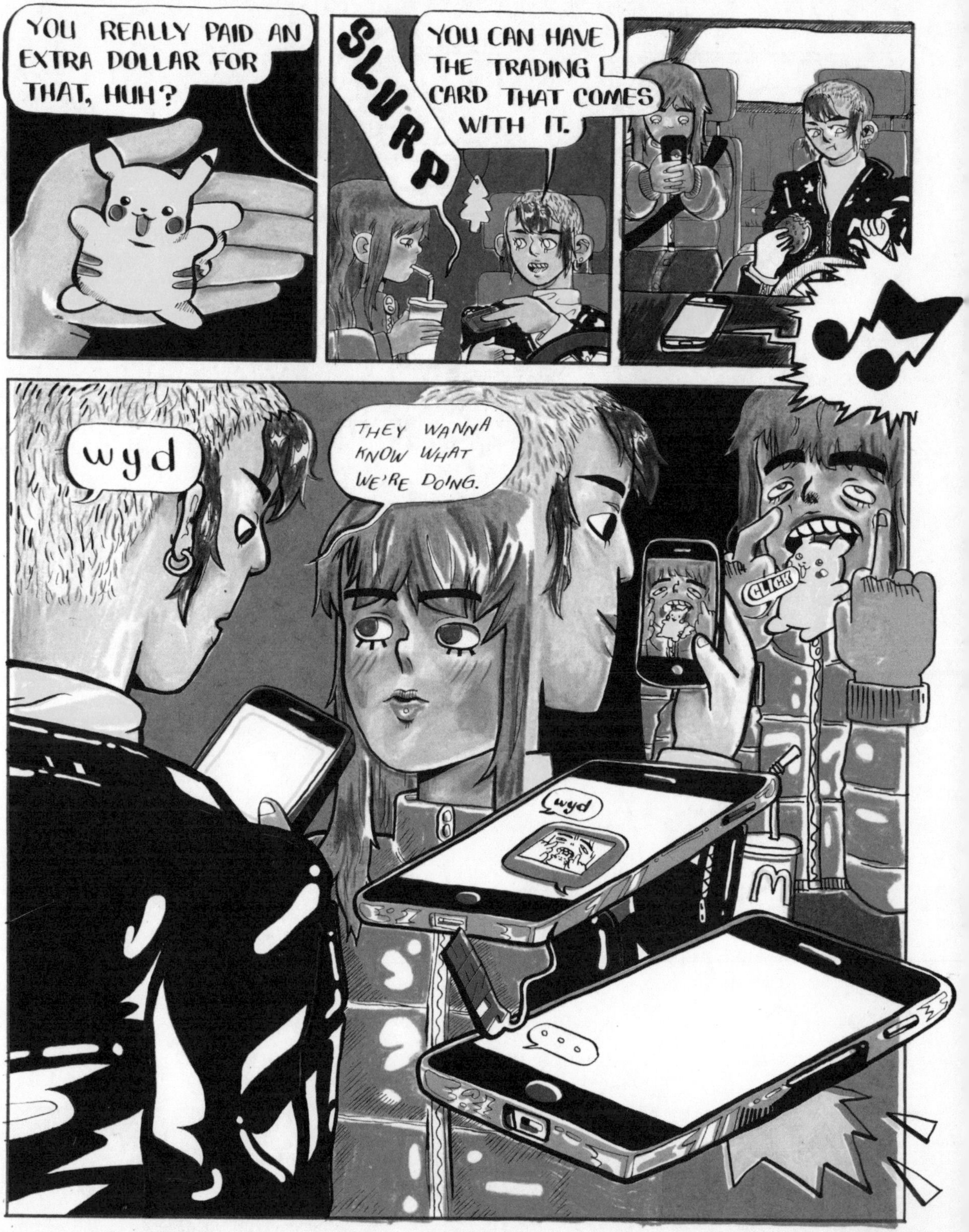
YOU REALLY PAID AN EXTRA DOLLAR FOR THAT, HUH?
SLURP
YOU CAN HAVE THE TRADING CARD THAT COMES WITH IT.
wyd
THEY WANNA KNOW WHAT WE'RE DOING.
CLICK
wyd
...

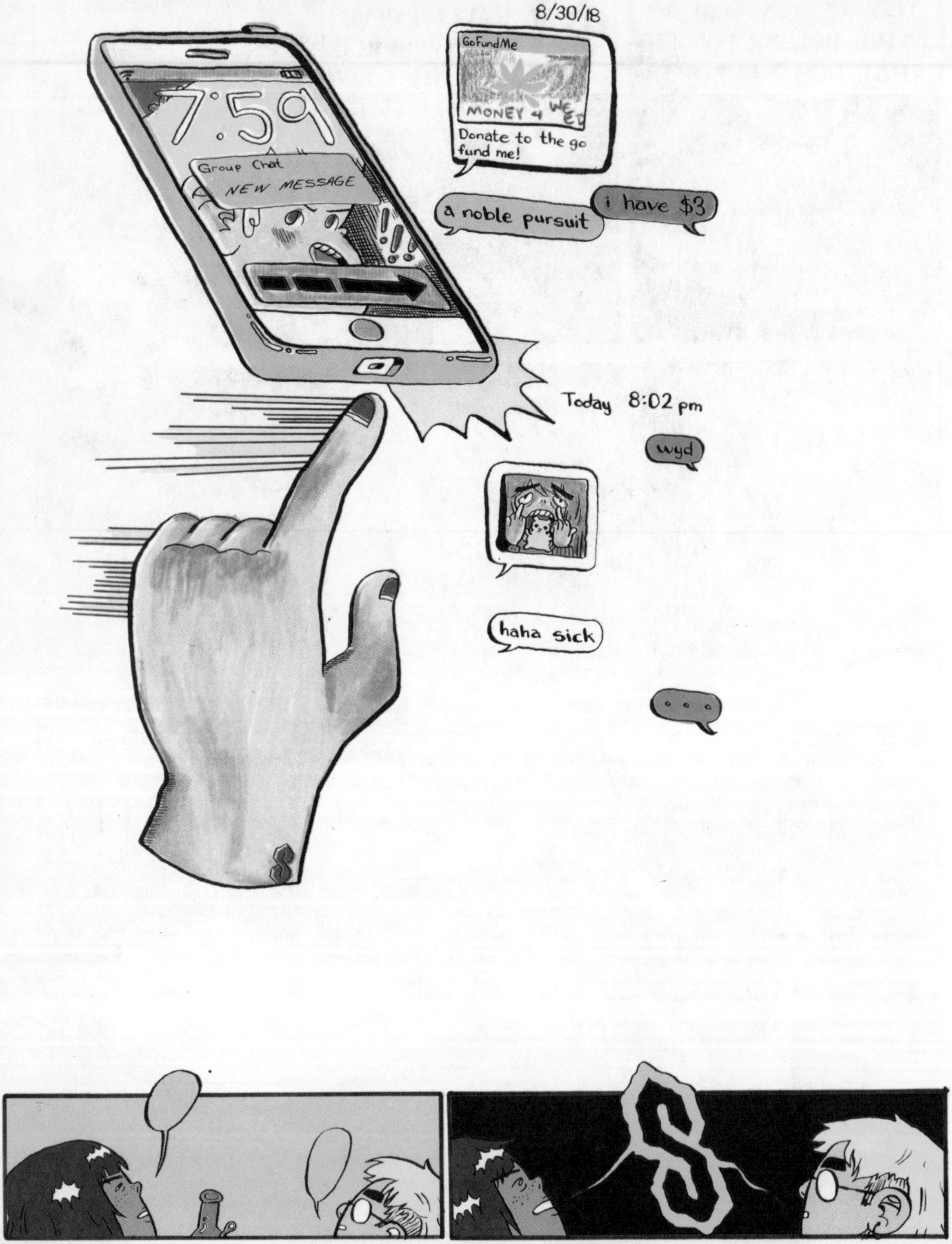
7:59
Group Chat
NEW MESSAGE
8/30/18
GoFundMe
MONEY 4 WEED
Donate to the go fund me!
a noble pursuit
i have $3
Today 8:02 pm
wyd
haha sick
• • •

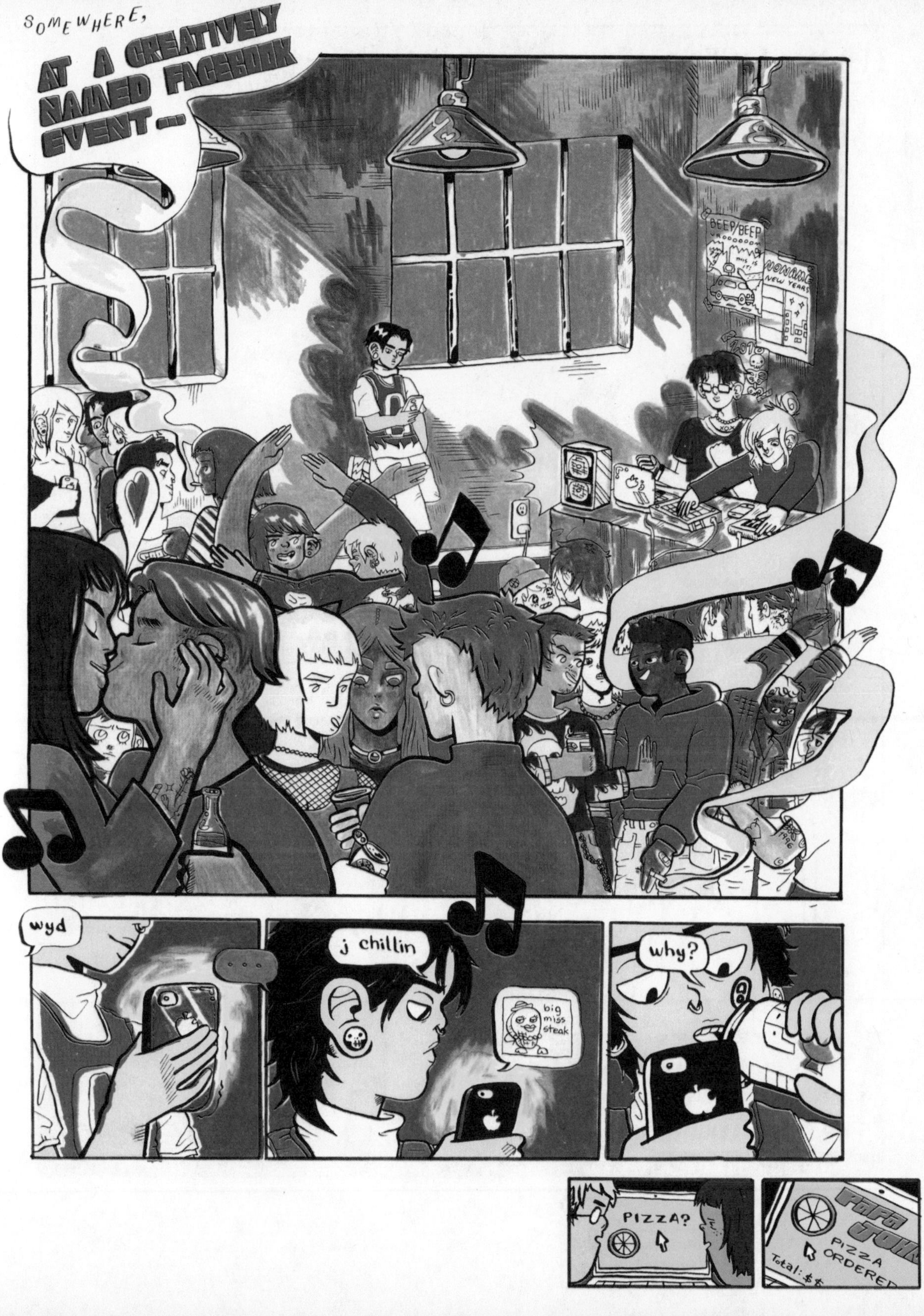

SOMEWHERE,
AT A CREATIVELY NAMED FACEBOOK EVENT...
BEEP/BEEP
NONAME NEW YEARS
wyd
...
j chillin
big miss steak
why?
PIZZA?
PIZZA ORDERED
Total: $$

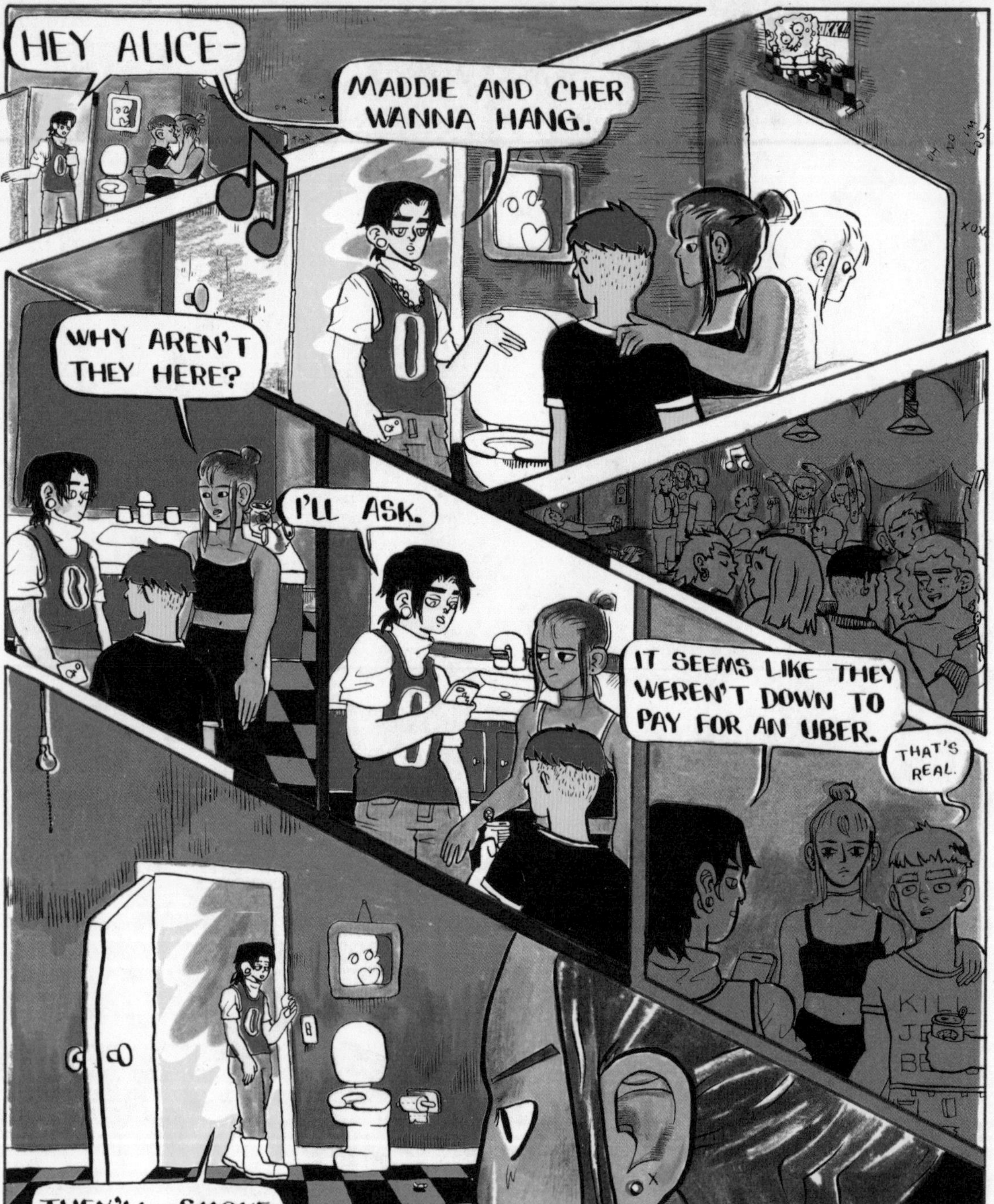
HEY ALICE-
MADDIE AND CHER WANNA HANG.
WHY AREN'T THEY HERE?
I'LL ASK.
IT SEEMS LIKE THEY WEREN'T DOWN TO PAY FOR AN UBER.
THAT'S REAL.
THEY'LL SMOKE US OUT IF WE GO TO THEIRS.

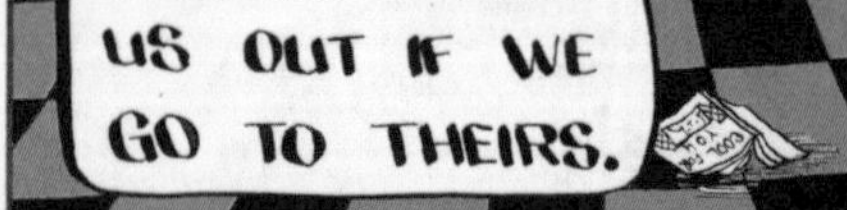
PIZZA
TRACKER
BEING MADE
00:45:03 MINUTES REMAINING

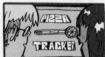

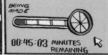

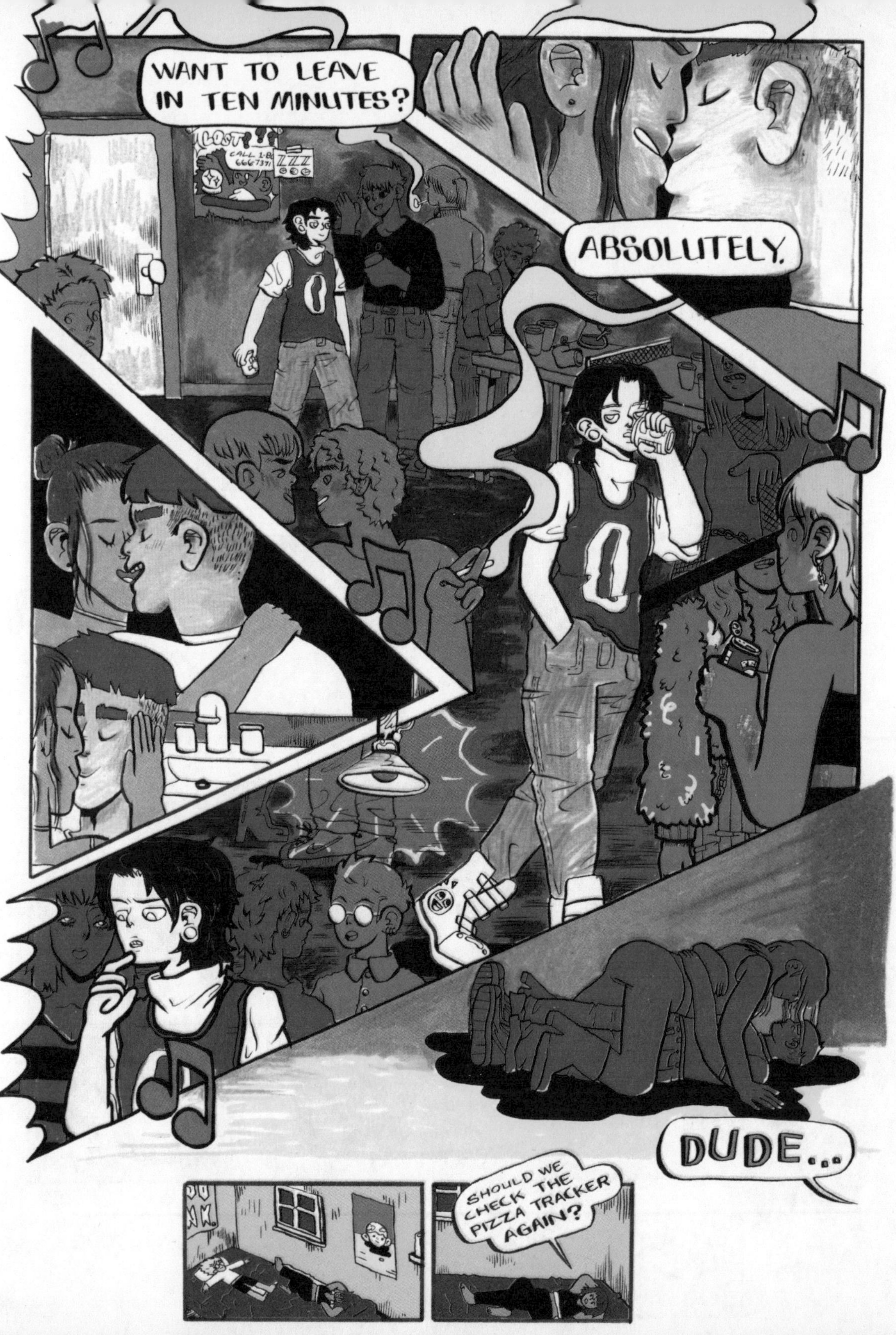
WANT TO LEAVE IN TEN MINUTES?
LOST
ABSOLUTELY.
DUDE...
SHOULD WE CHECK THE PIZZA TRACKER AGAIN?

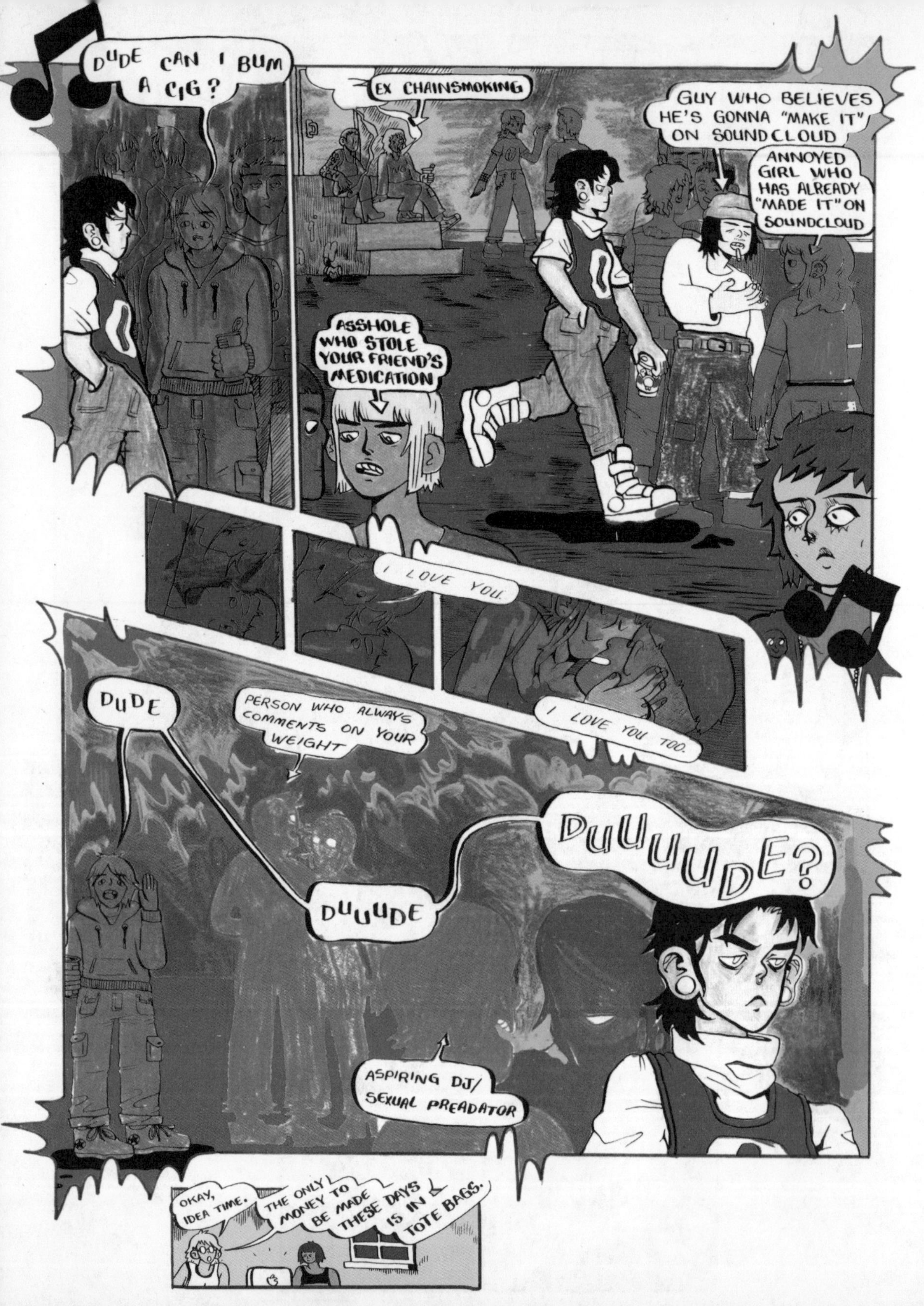
DUDE CAN I BUM A CIG?
EX CHAINSMOKING
GUY WHO BELIEVES HE'S GONNA "MAKE IT" ON SOUNDCLOUD
ANNOYED GIRL WHO HAS ALREADY "MADE IT" ON SOUNDCLOUD
ASSHOLE WHO STOLE YOUR FRIEND'S MEDICATION
I LOVE YOU.
I LOVE YOU TOO.
DUDE
PERSON WHO ALWAYS COMMENTS ON YOUR WEIGHT
DUUUDE
DUUUUDE?
ASPIRING DJ/ SEXUAL PREADATOR
OKAY, IDEA TIME.
THE ONLY MONEY TO BE MADE THESE DAYS IS IN TOTE BAGS.

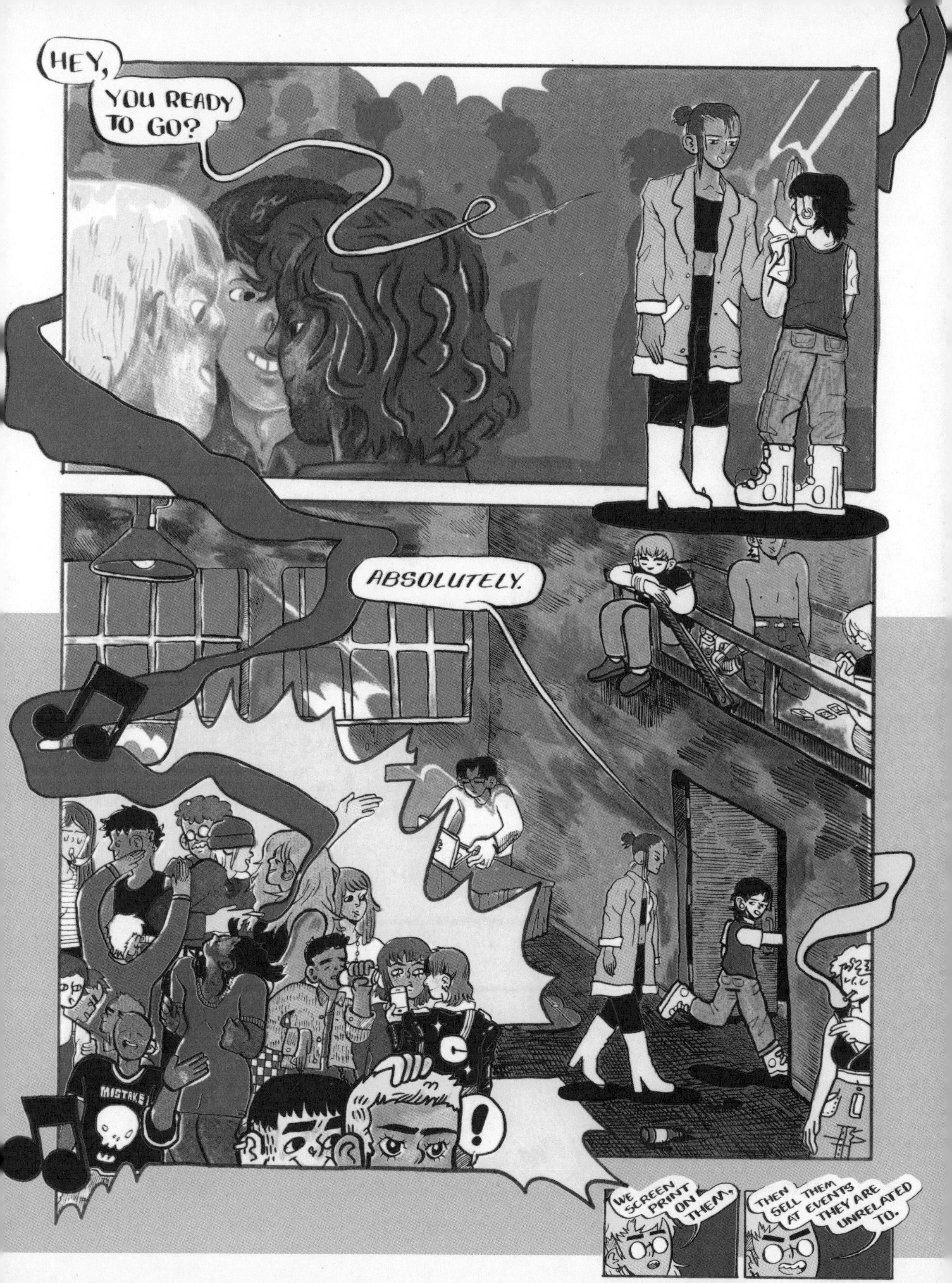
HEY,
YOU READY TO GO?
ABSOLUTELY.
WE SCREEN PRINT ON THEM,
THEN SELL THEM AT EVENTS THEY ARE UNRELATED TO.

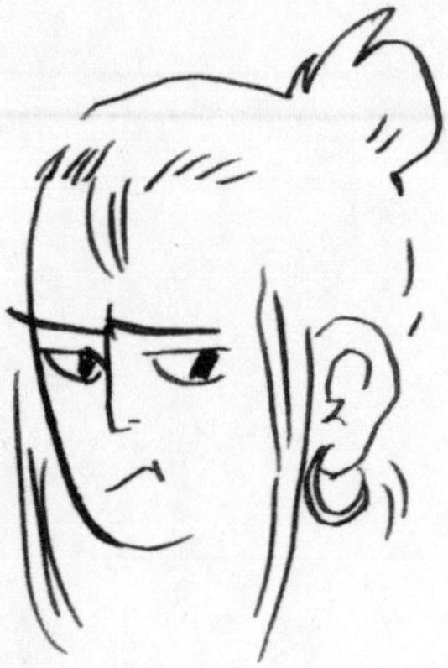

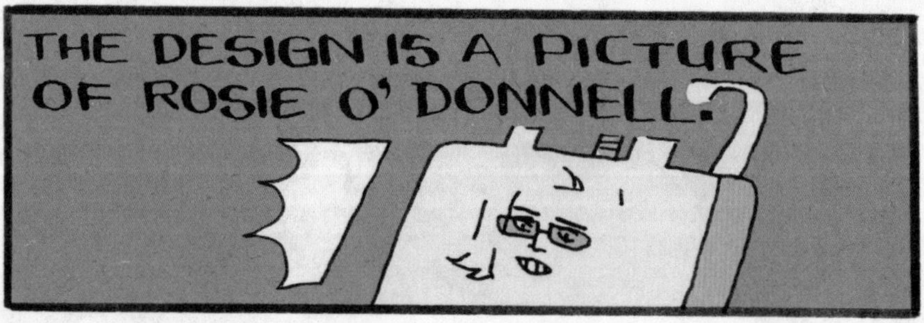

THE DESIGN IS A PICTURE OF ROSIE O' DONNELL.

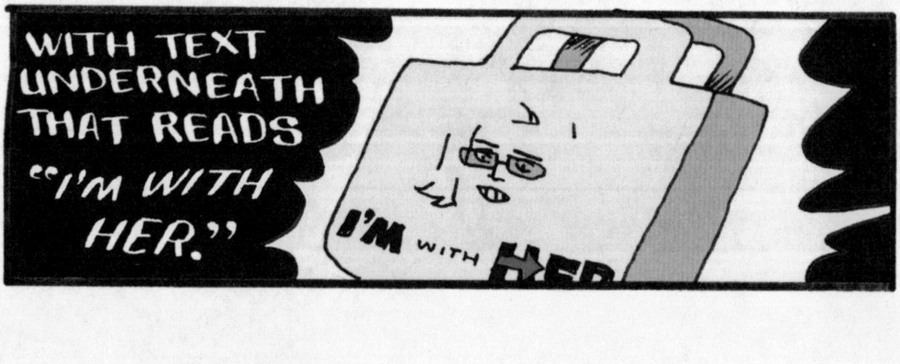

WITH TEXT UNDERNEATH THAT READS "I'M WITH HER."
I'M WITH

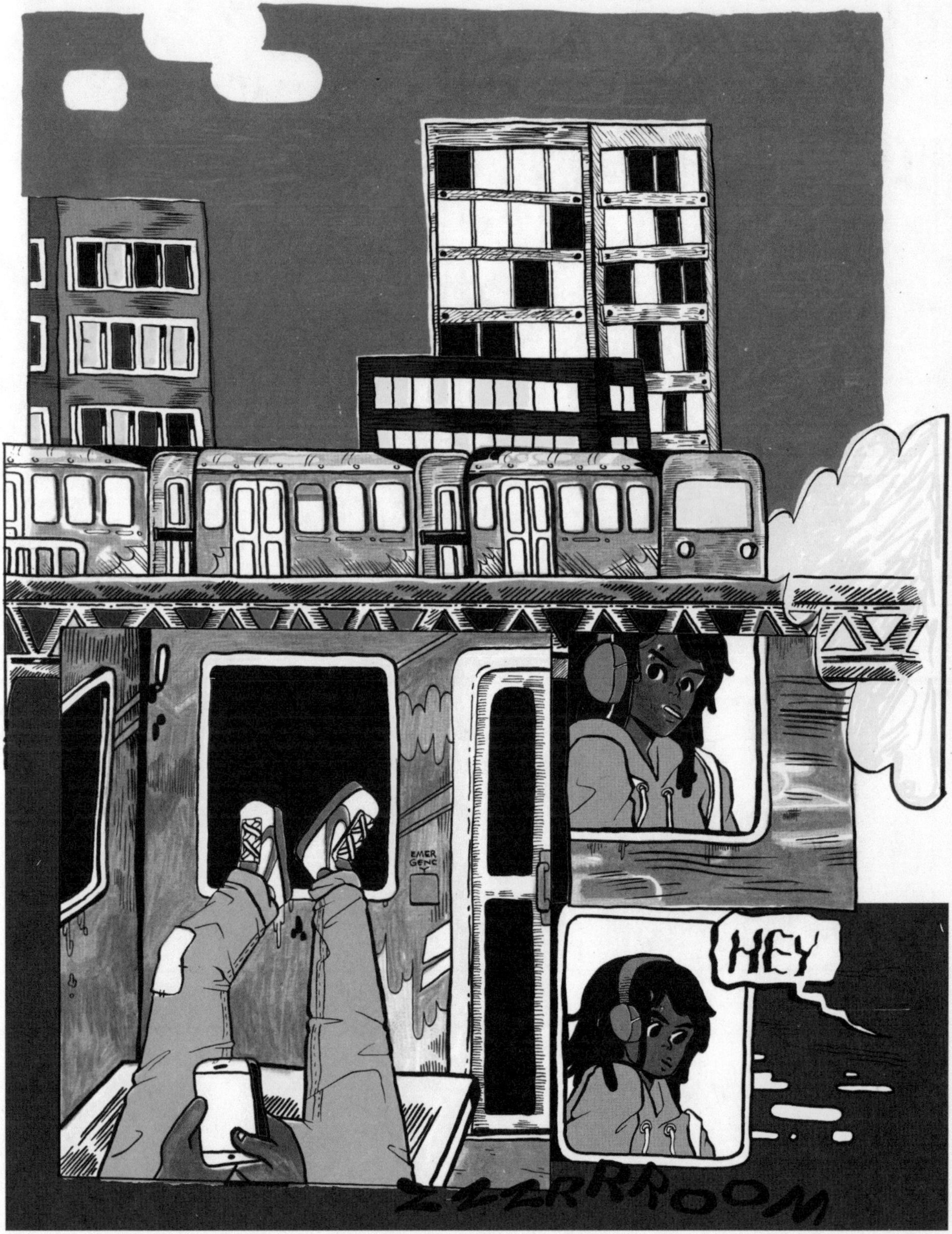
EMER
GENC
HEY
ZZZRRROOM

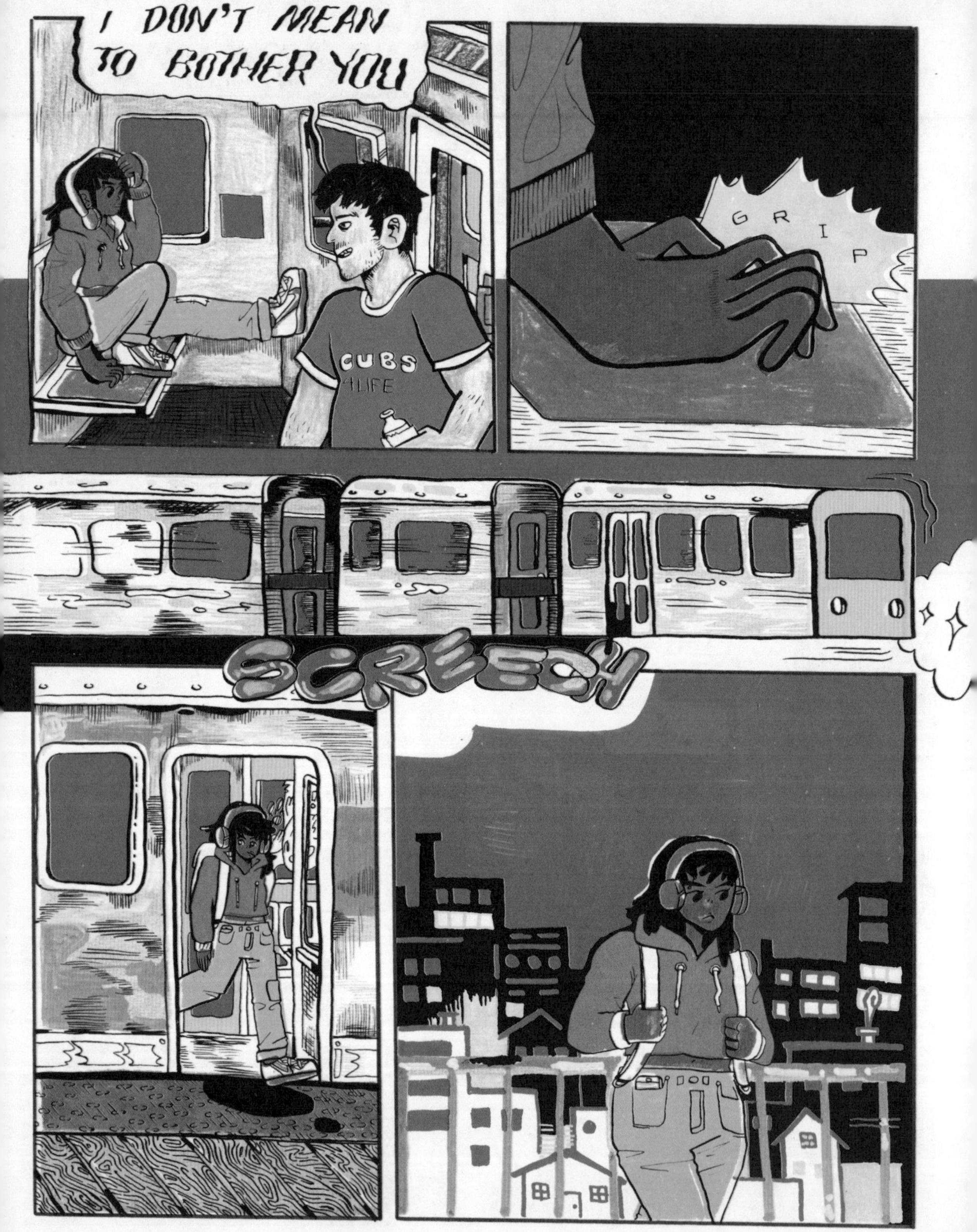
I DON'T MEAN TO BOTHER YOU
CUBS 4LIFE
GRIP
SCREECH

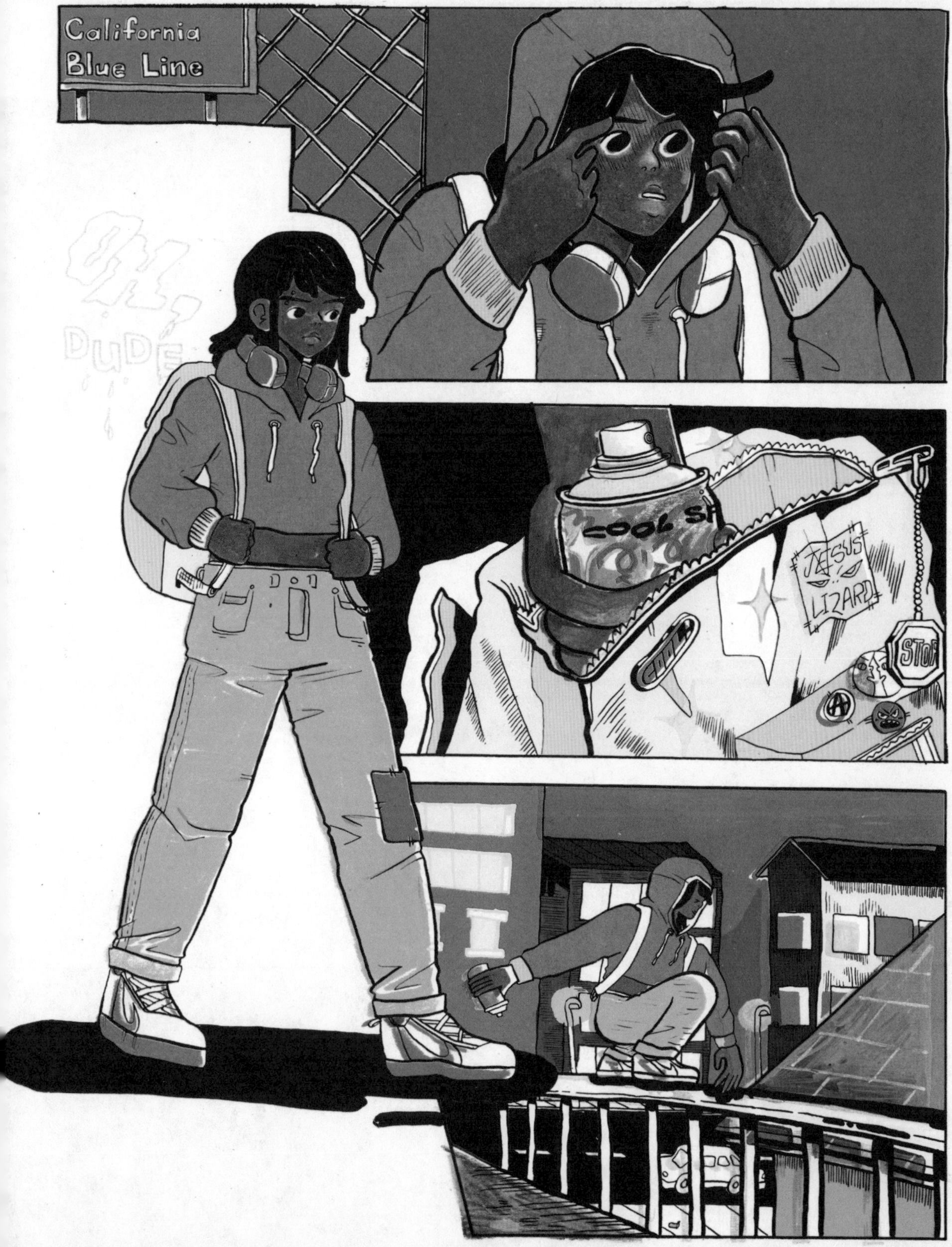
California
Blue Line
OH,
DUDE
COOL SP
JESUS
LIZARD
STOP

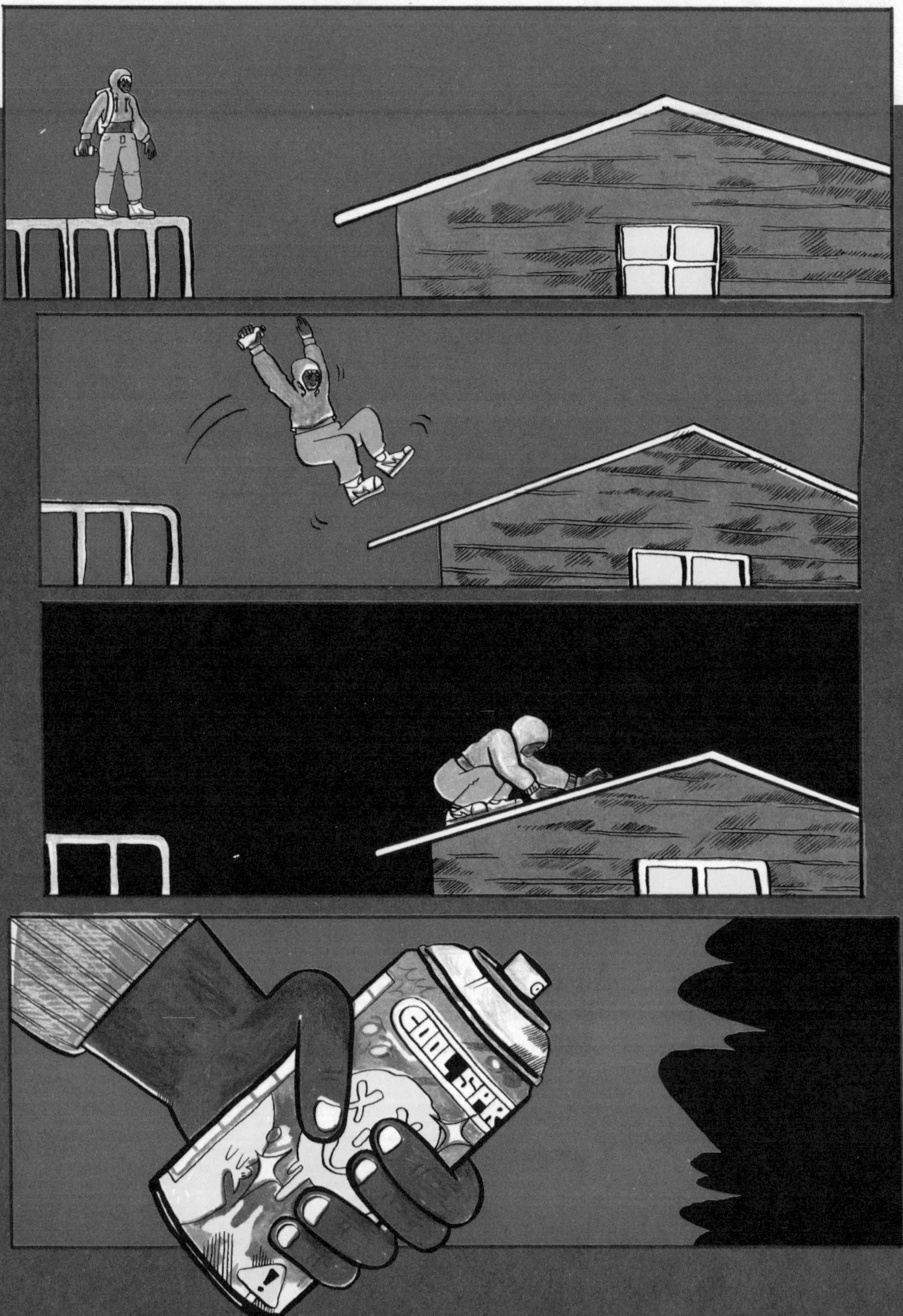
COOL SPR

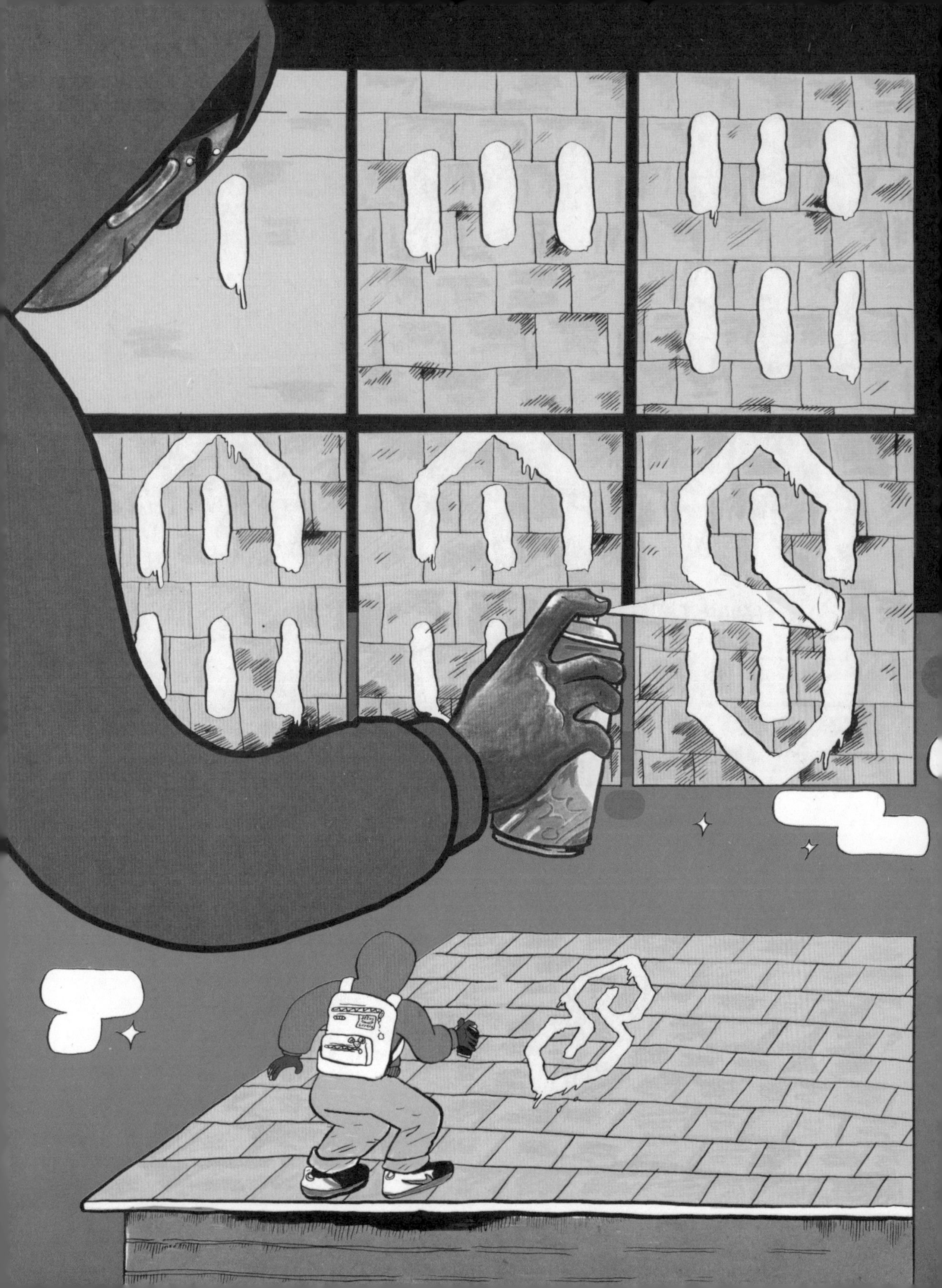

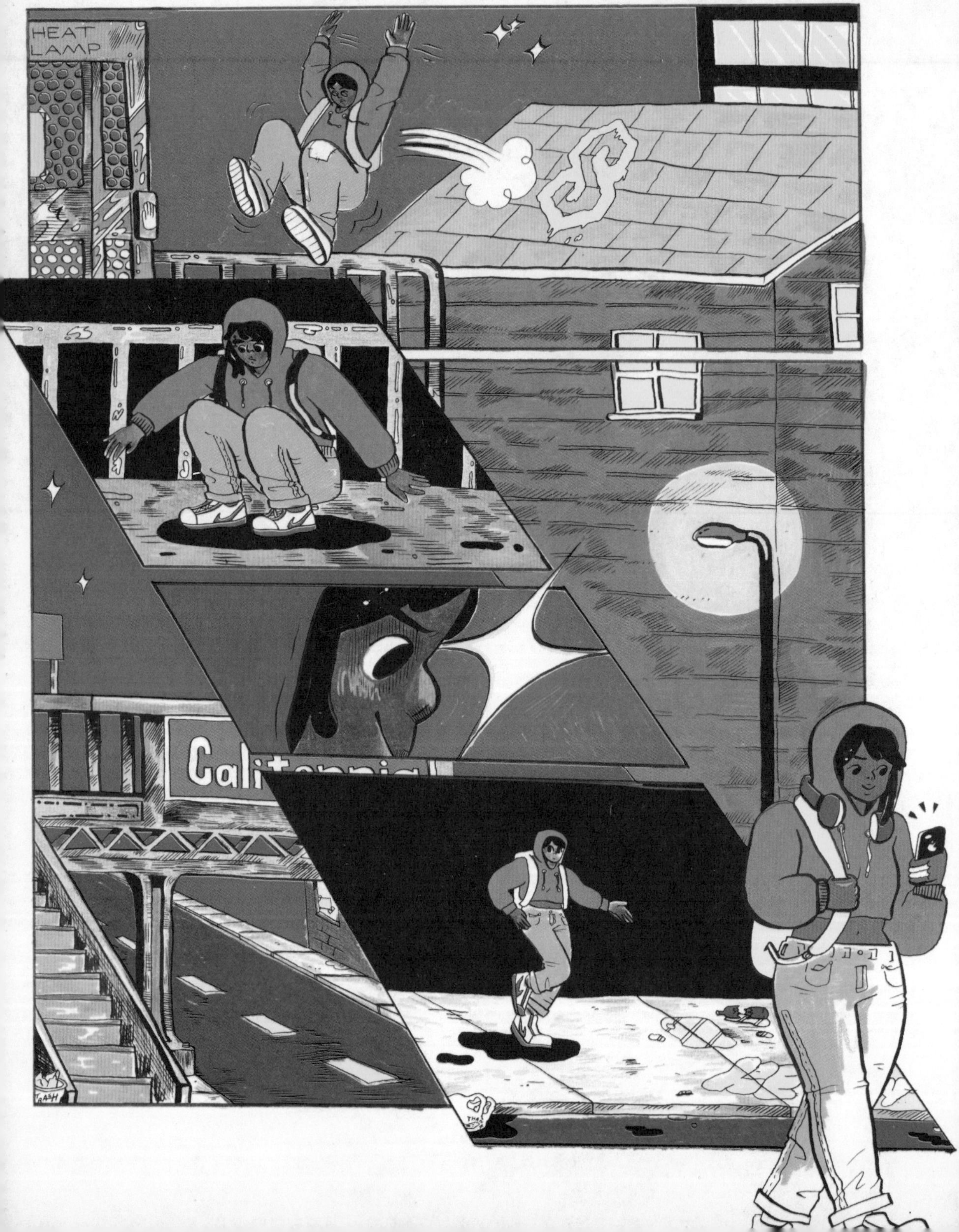
HEAT
LAMP
TRASH

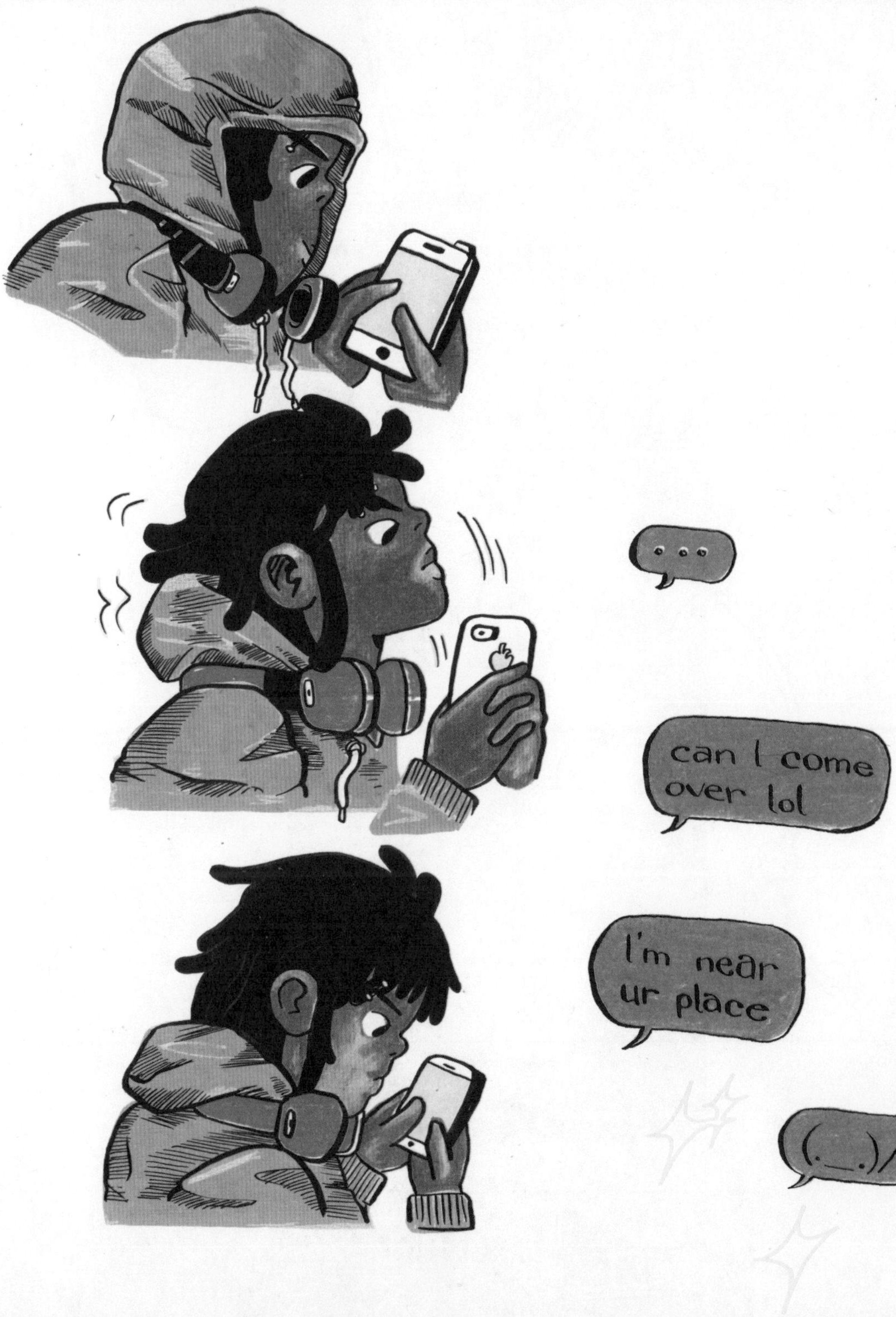
• • •
can I come over lol
I'm near ur place
(._.)/

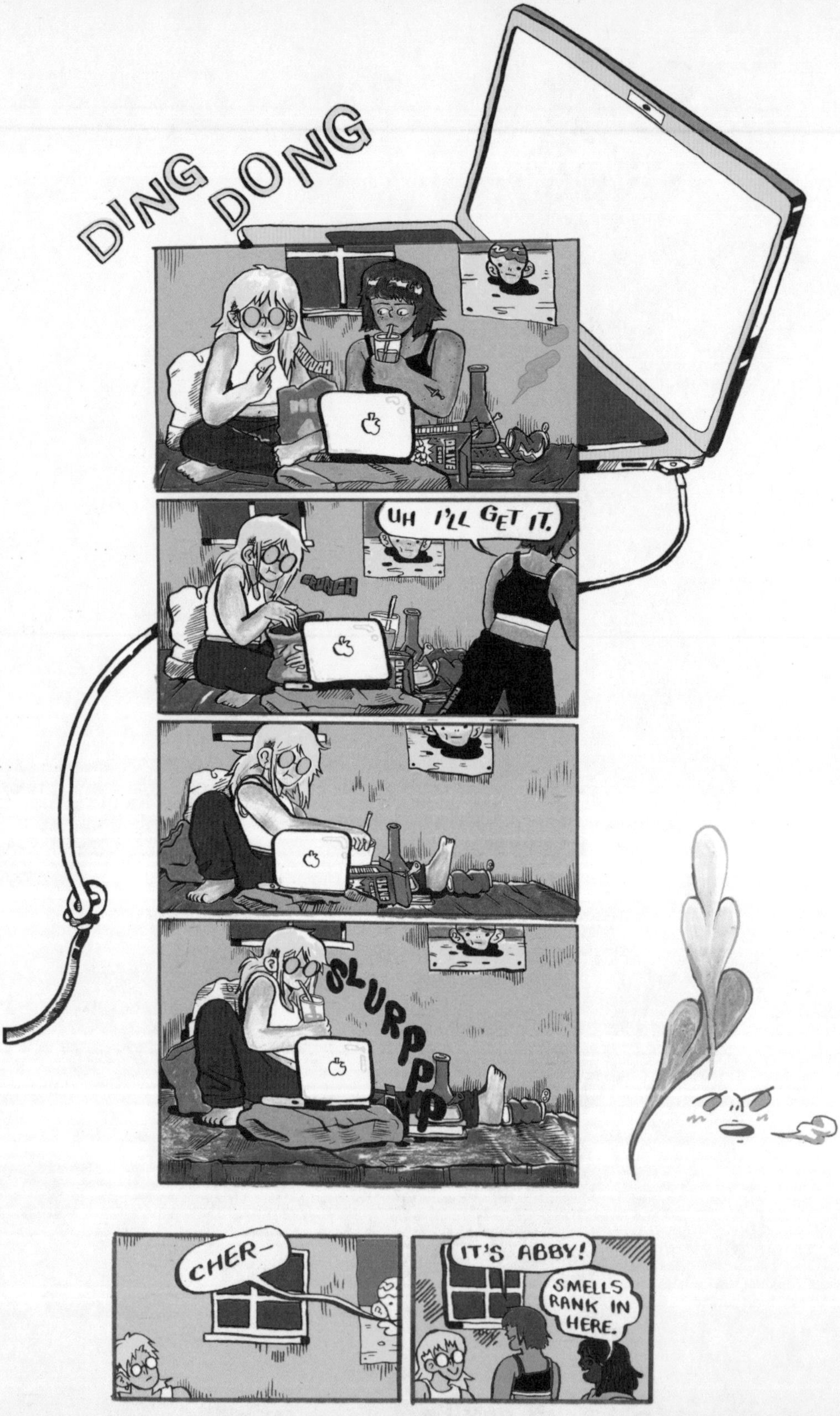
DING DONG
MUNCH
UH I'LL GET IT.
CRUNCH
SLURPPP
CHER-
IT'S ABBY!
SMELLS RANK IN HERE.

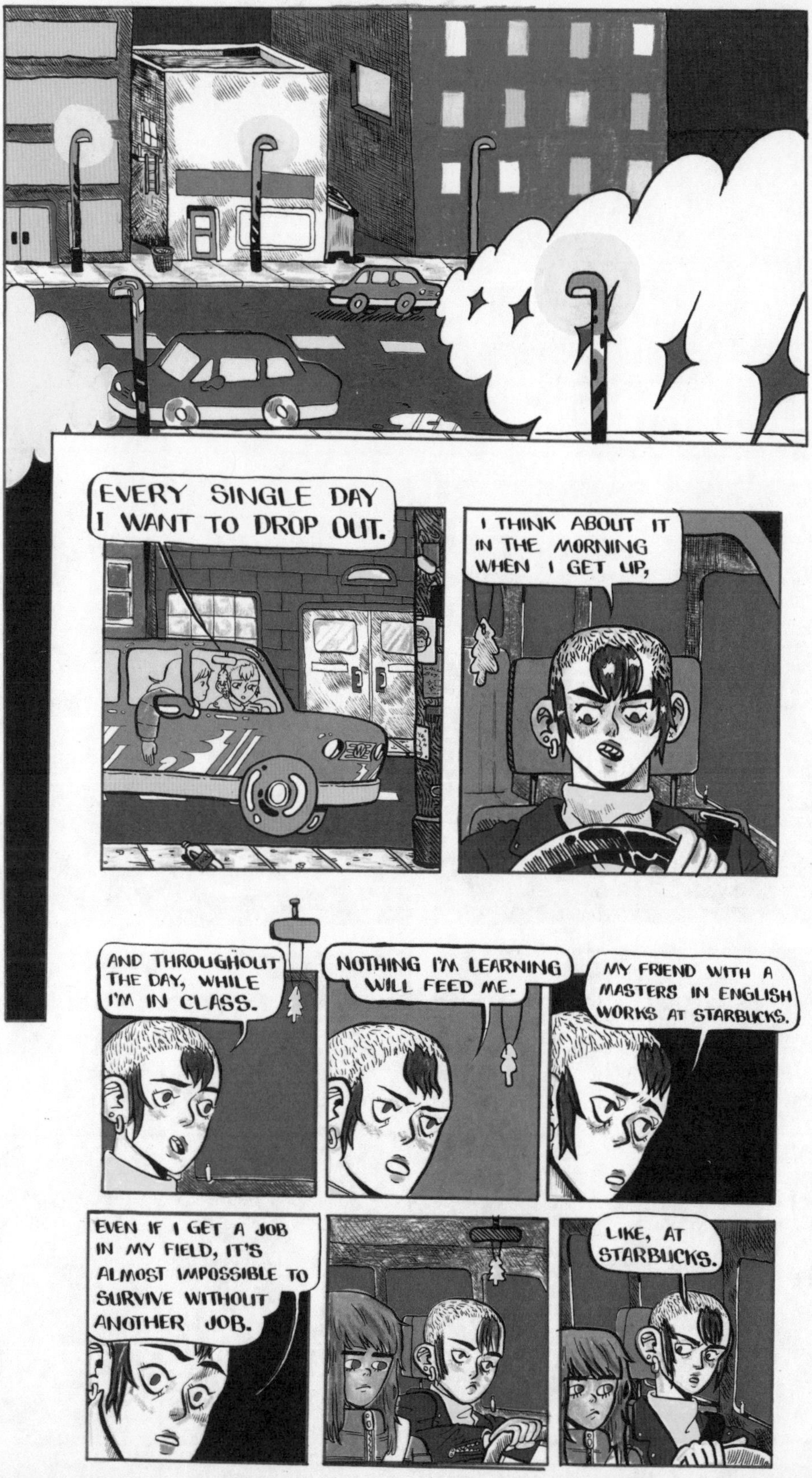
EVERY SINGLE DAY I WANT TO DROP OUT.
I THINK ABOUT IT IN THE MORNING WHEN I GET UP,
AND THROUGHOUT THE DAY, WHILE I'M IN CLASS.
NOTHING I'M LEARNING WILL FEED ME.
MY FRIEND WITH A MASTERS IN ENGLISH WORKS AT STARBUCKS.
EVEN IF I GET A JOB IN MY FIELD, IT'S ALMOST IMPOSSIBLE TO SURVIVE WITHOUT ANOTHER JOB.
LIKE, AT STARBUCKS.

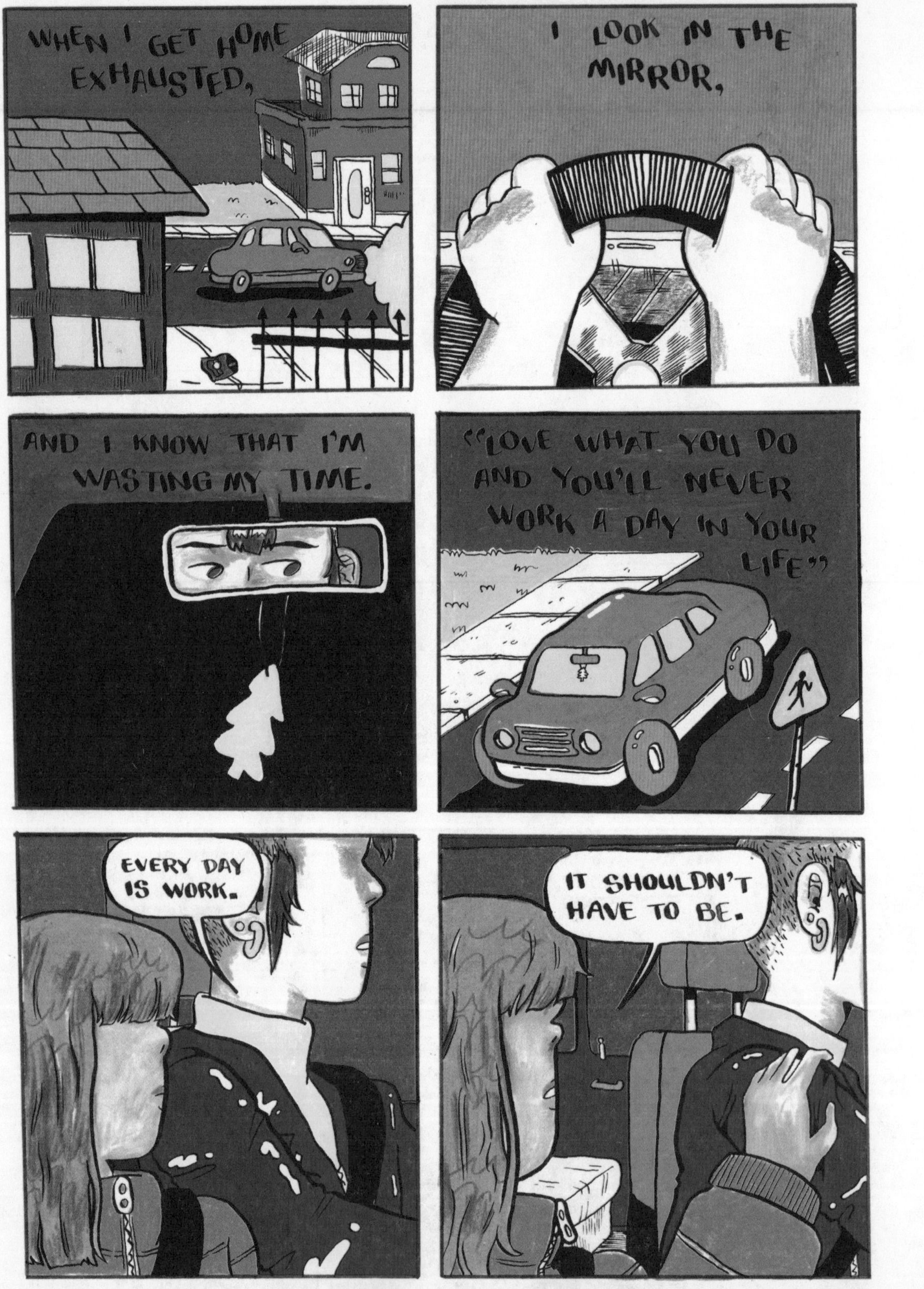
WHEN I GET HOME EXHAUSTED,
I LOOK IN THE MIRROR,
AND I KNOW THAT I'M WASTING MY TIME.
"LOVE WHAT YOU DO AND YOU'LL NEVER WORK A DAY IN YOUR LIFE"
EVERY DAY IS WORK.
IT SHOULDN'T HAVE TO BE.

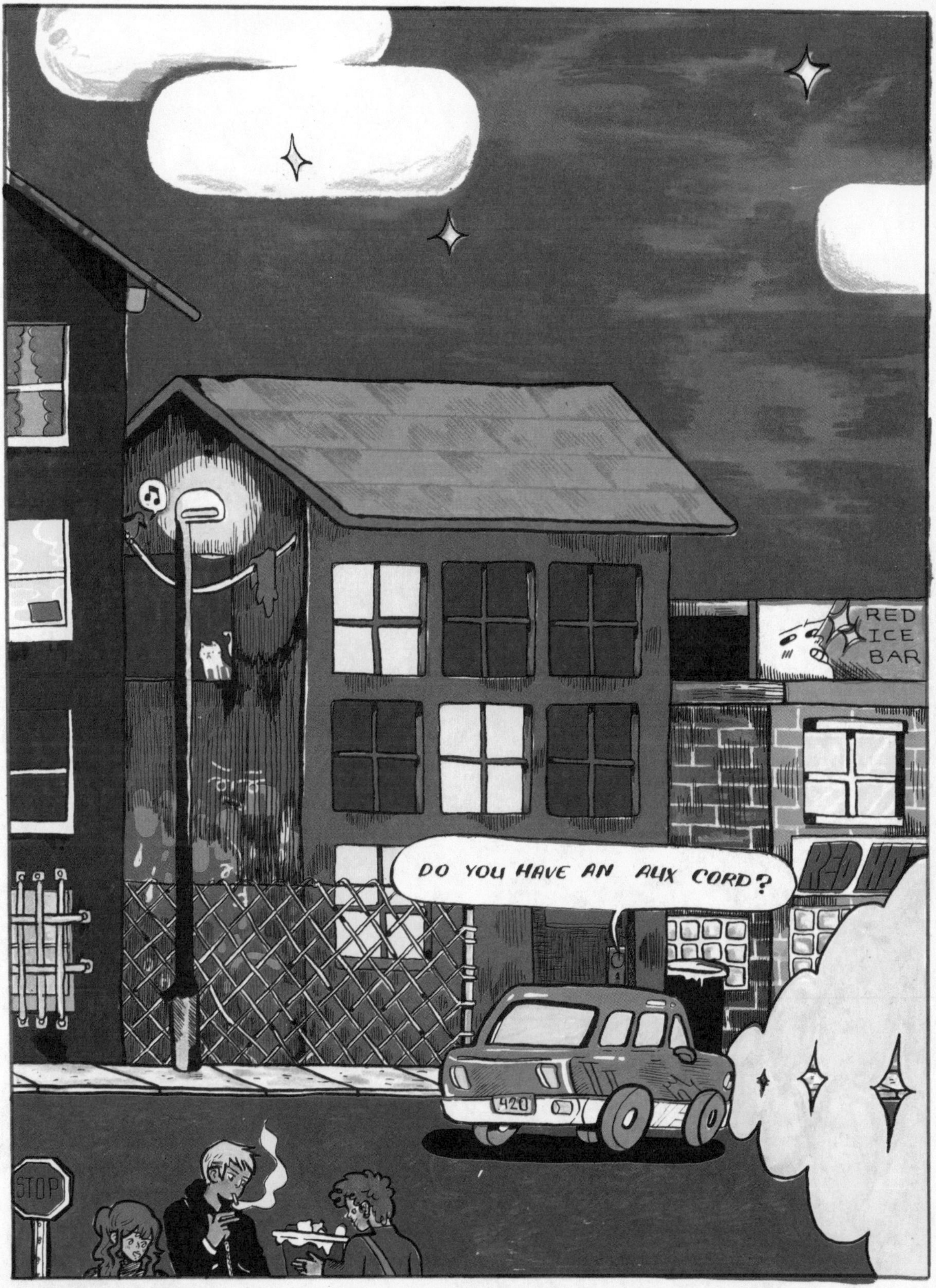
RED
ICE
BAR
DO YOU HAVE AN AUX CORD?
420
STOP

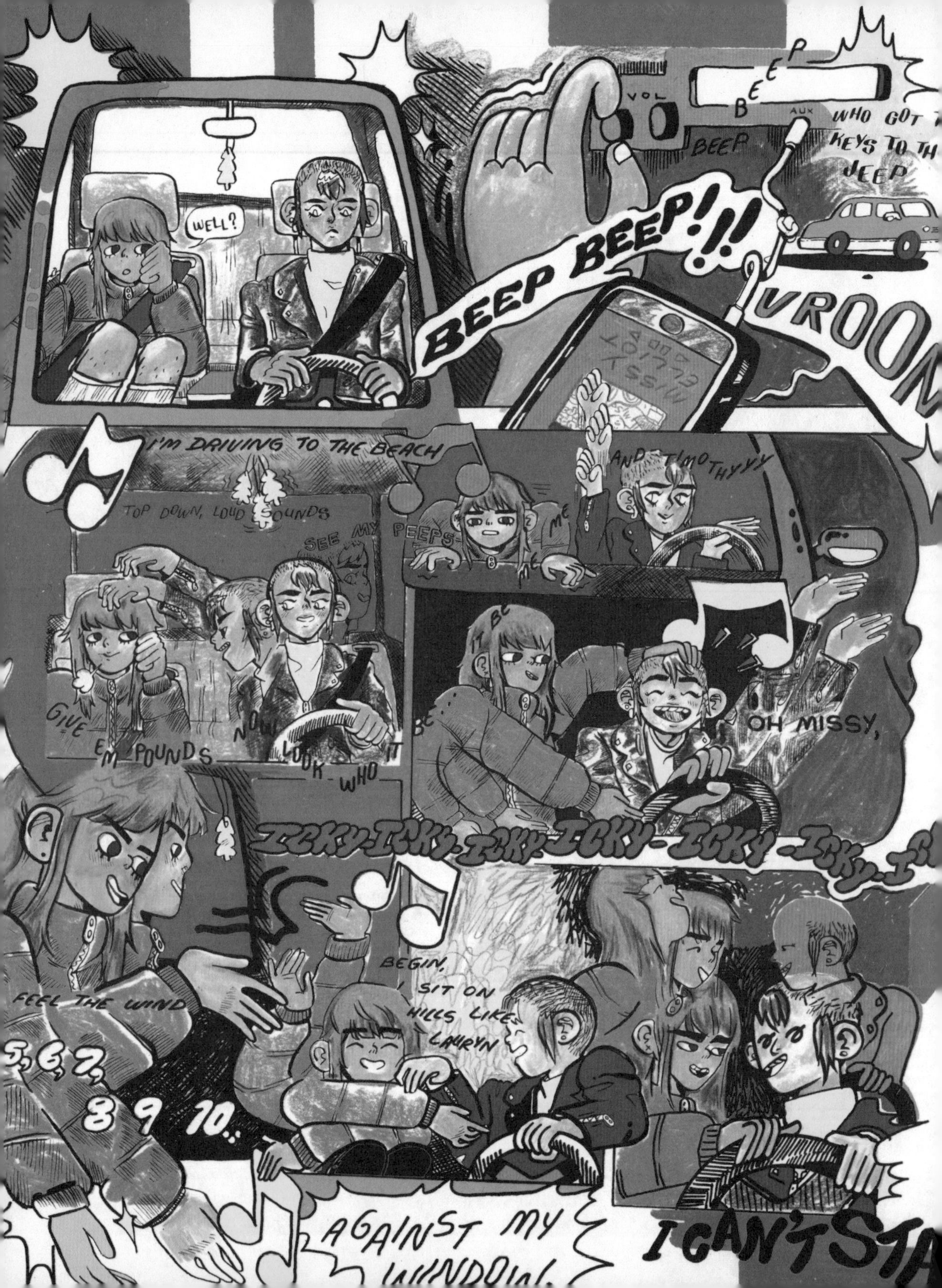

WELL?
VOL
AUX
BEEP
BEEP
WHO GOT KEYS TO TH JEEP
BEEP BEEP!!!
MISSY ELLIOT
VROOM
I'M DRIVING TO THE BEACH
TOP DOWN, LOUD SOUNDS
SEE MY PEEPS
ME
AND TIMOTHYYY
GIVE EM POUNDS
NOW LOOK WHO IT
WHO
IT BE
BE
OH MISSY,
ICKY-ICKY-ICKY-ICKY-ICKY-ICKY-I
FEEL THE WIND
5, 6, 7, 8 9 10..
BEGIN, I SIT ON HILLS LIKE LAURYN
AGAINST MY WINDOW.
I CAN'T STA

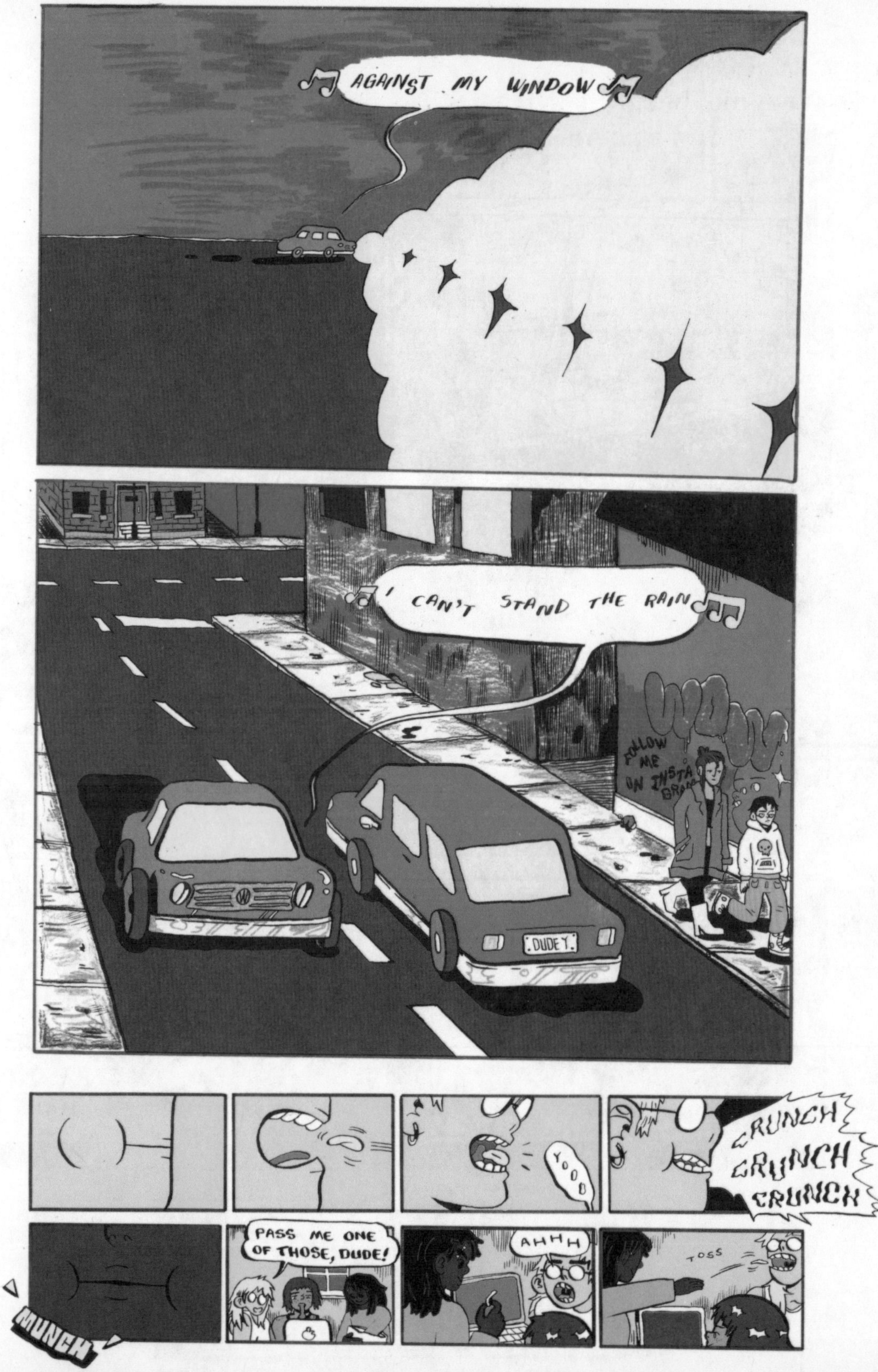
AGAINST MY WINDOW
I CAN'T STAND THE RAIN
FOLLOW ME ON INSTAGRAM
DUDEY
YOOO
CRUNCH CRUNCH CRUNCH
MUNCH
PASS ME ONE OF THOSE, DUDE!
AHHH
TOSS

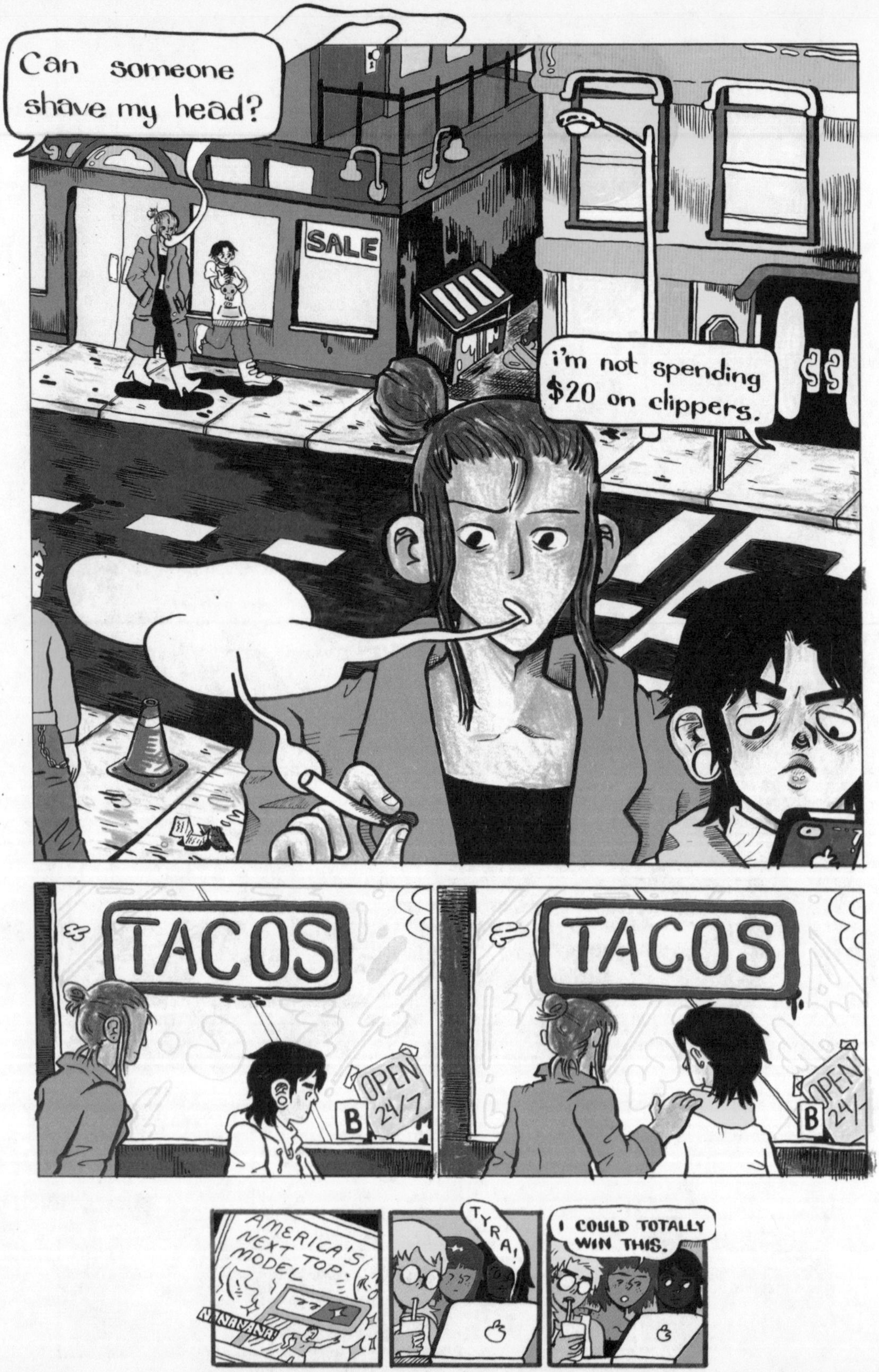
Can someone shave my head?
i'm not spending $20 on clippers.
TACOS
OPEN 24/7
TACOS
AMERICA'S NEXT TOP MODEL
TYRA!
I COULD TOTALLY WIN THIS.

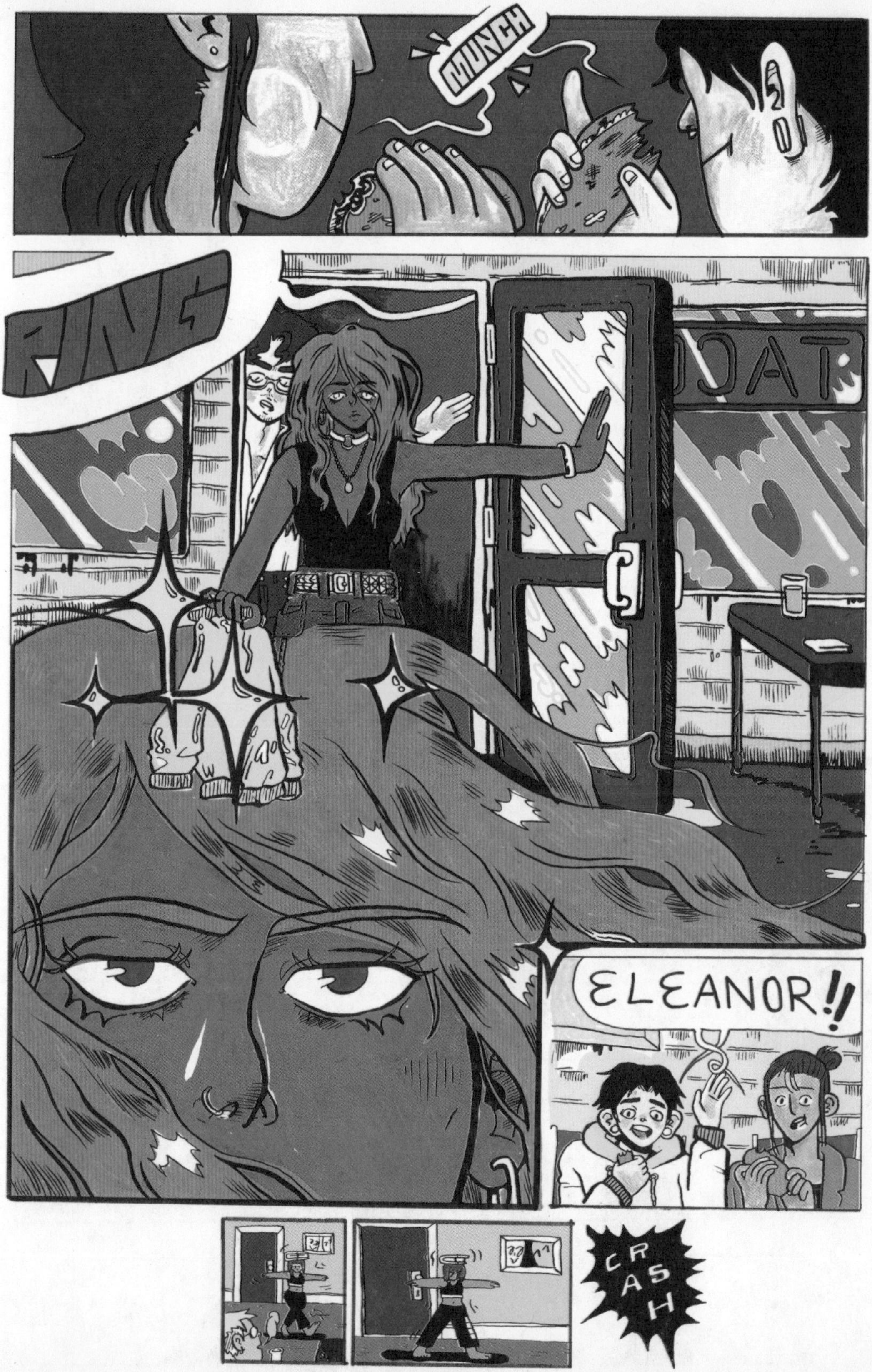
MUNCH
RING
TACO
ELEANOR!!
CRASH

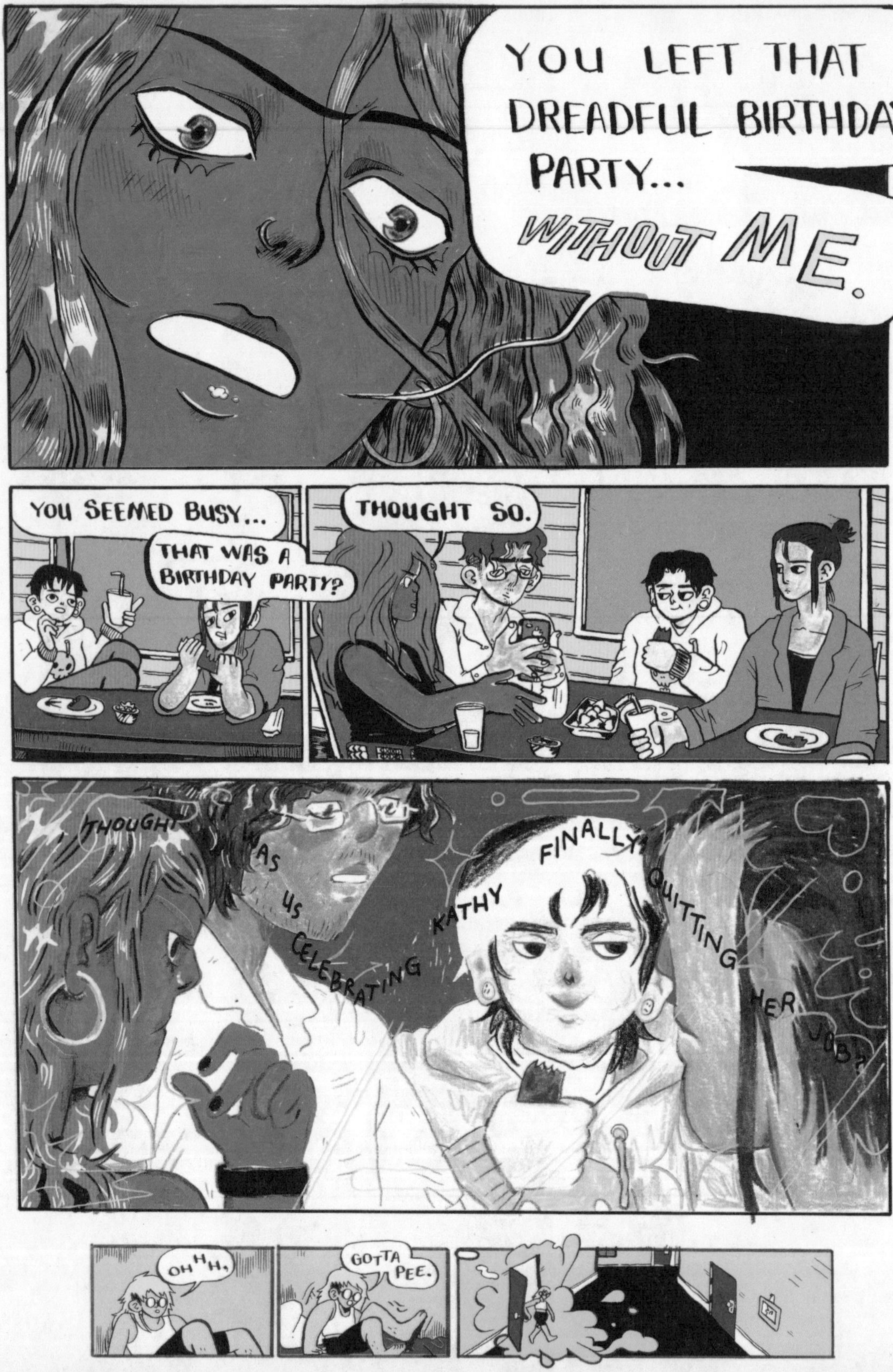
YOU LEFT THAT DREADFUL BIRTHDAY PARTY... WITHOUT ME.
YOU SEEMED BUSY...
THAT WAS A BIRTHDAY PARTY?
THOUGHT SO.
THOUGHT IT WAS US CELEBRATING KATHY FINALLY QUITTING HER JOB?
OHHH,
GOTTA PEE.

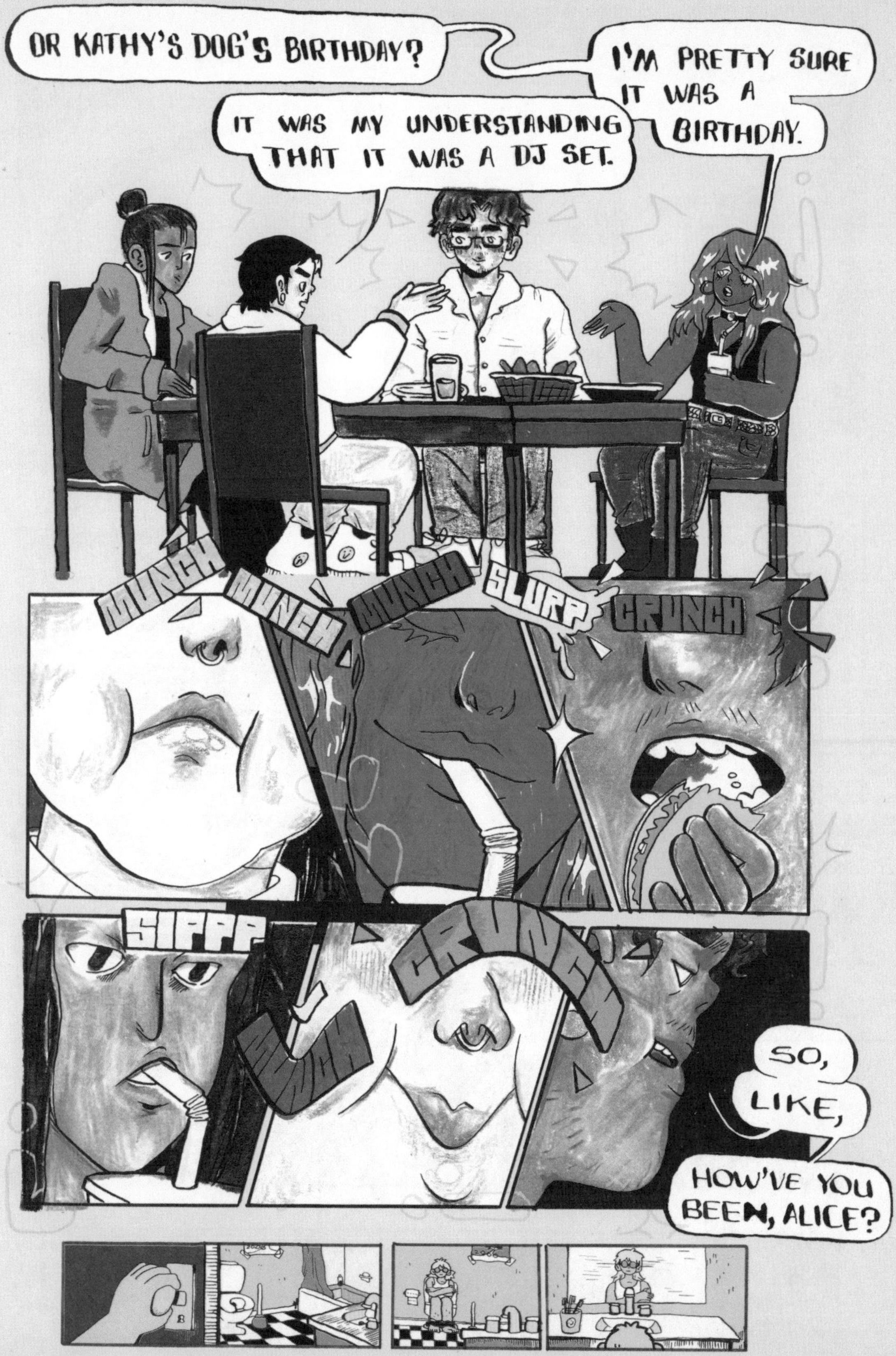
OR KATHY'S DOG'S BIRTHDAY?
IT WAS MY UNDERSTANDING THAT IT WAS A DJ SET.
I'M PRETTY SURE IT WAS A BIRTHDAY.
MUNCH
MUNCH
MUNCH
SLURP
CRUNCH
SIPPP
MUNCH
CRUNCH
SO, LIKE,
HOW'VE YOU BEEN, ALICE?

WHAT DO YOU MEAN?
Y'KNOW, ALL THAT STUFF
WITH YOUR BOSS.
CHER SAID YOU WERE HAVING A ROUGH TIME.
I WAS.
BUT I QUIT.

SHOULD I SHAVE MY HEAD?

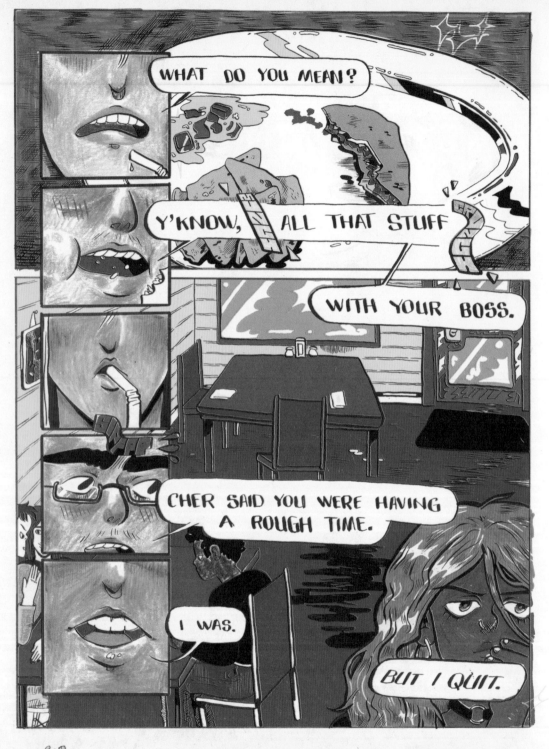

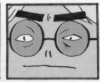

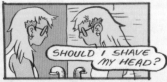

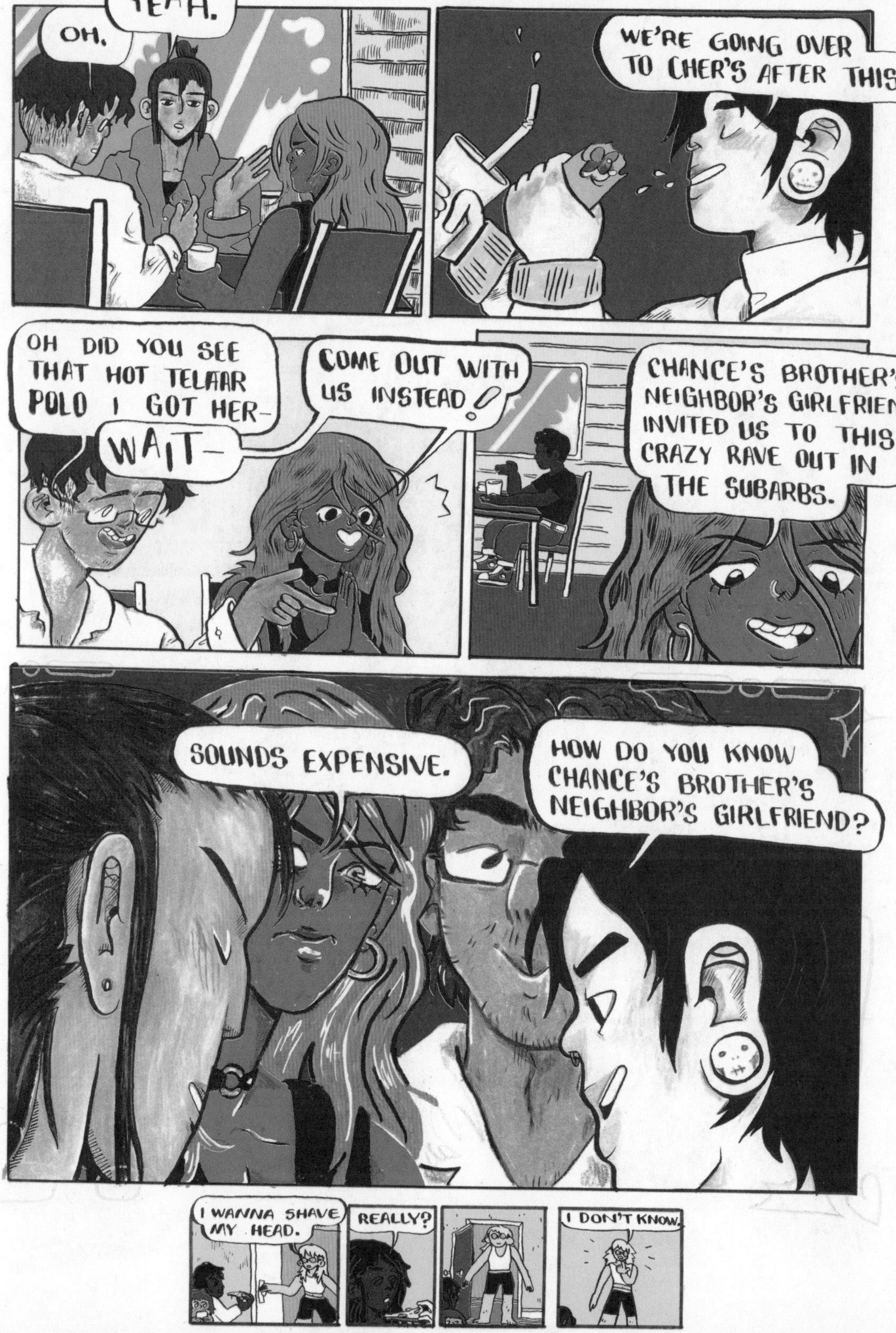
OH.
YEAH.
WE'RE GOING OVER TO CHER'S AFTER THIS!
OH DID YOU SEE THAT HOT TELAAR POLO I GOT HER-
WAIT-
COME OUT WITH US INSTEAD!
CHANCE'S BROTHER'S NEIGHBOR'S GIRLFRIEND INVITED US TO THIS CRAZY RAVE OUT IN THE SUBARBS.
SOUNDS EXPENSIVE.
HOW DO YOU KNOW CHANCE'S BROTHER'S NEIGHBOR'S GIRLFRIEND?
I WANNA SHAVE MY HEAD.
REALLY?
I DON'T KNOW.

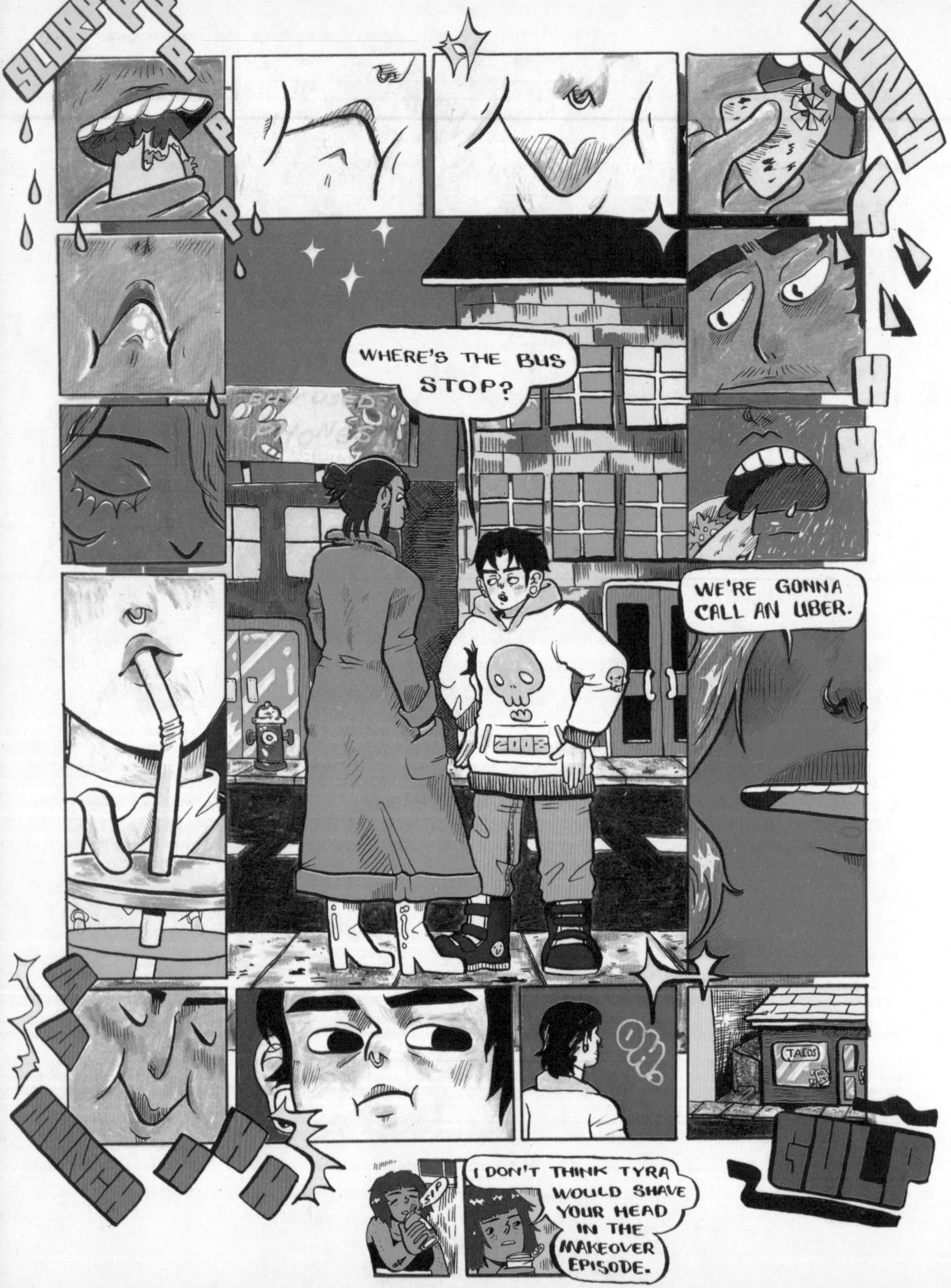
CRUNCH
WHERE'S THE BUS STOP?
WE'RE GONNA CALL AN UBER.
2003
OH.
TACOS
GULP
SIP
I DON'T THINK TYRA WOULD SHAVE YOUR HEAD IN THE MAKEOVER EPISODE.

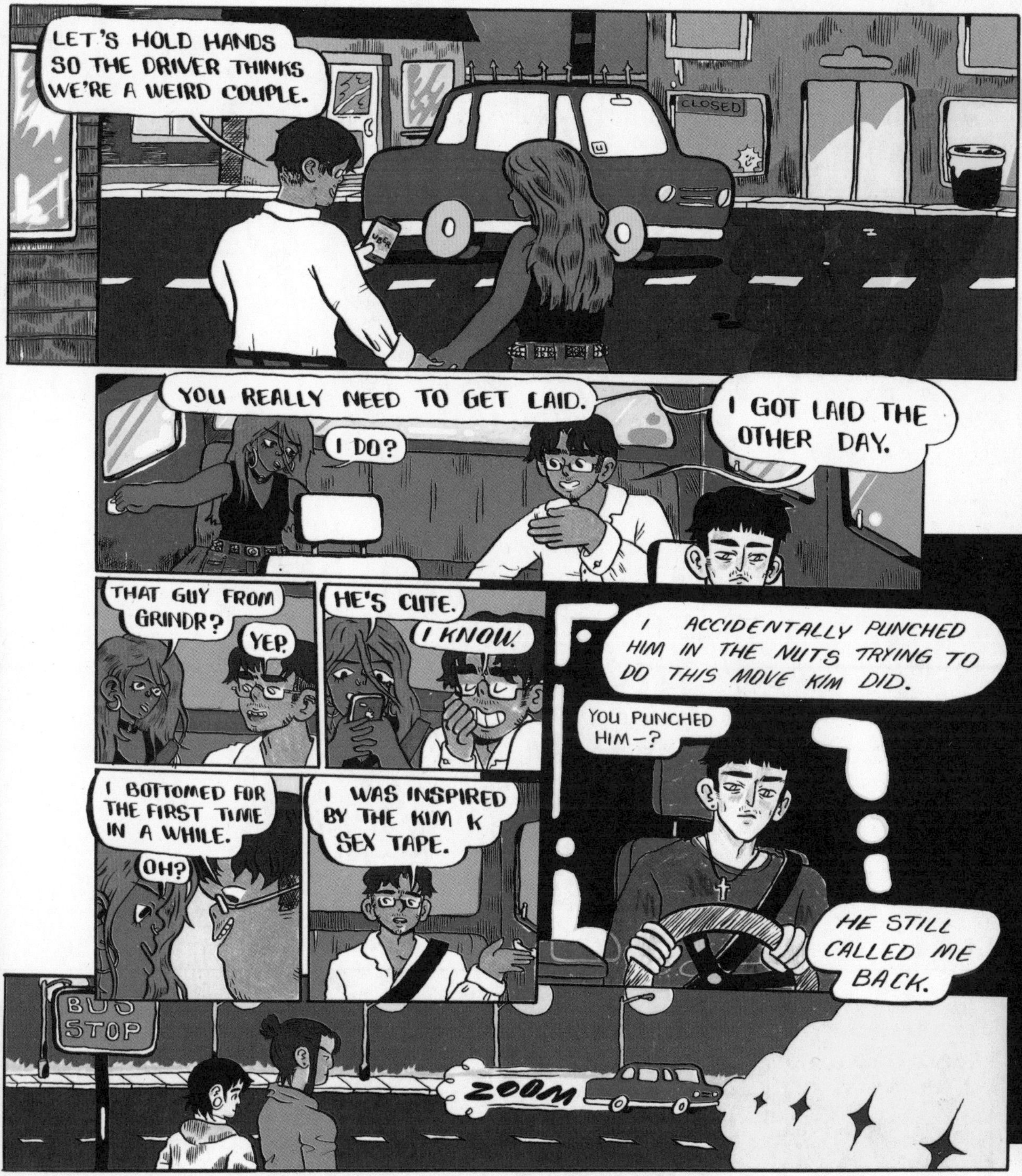
LET'S HOLD HANDS SO THE DRIVER THINKS WE'RE A WEIRD COUPLE.
UBER
CLOSED
YOU REALLY NEED TO GET LAID.
I DO?
I GOT LAID THE OTHER DAY.
THAT GUY FROM GRINDR?
YEP.
HE'S CUTE.
I KNOW.
I BOTTOMED FOR THE FIRST TIME IN A WHILE.
OH?
I WAS INSPIRED BY THE KIM K SEX TAPE.
I ACCIDENTALLY PUNCHED HIM IN THE NUTS TRYING TO DO THIS MOVE KIM DID.
YOU PUNCHED HIM-?
HE STILL CALLED ME BACK.
BUS STOP
ZOOM

YOU KNOW WHAT THEY SAY,

YOU EITHER DIE A HERO

OR LIVE LONG ENOUGH TO HAVE A FUNKO POP DOLL MADE OF YOURSELF.

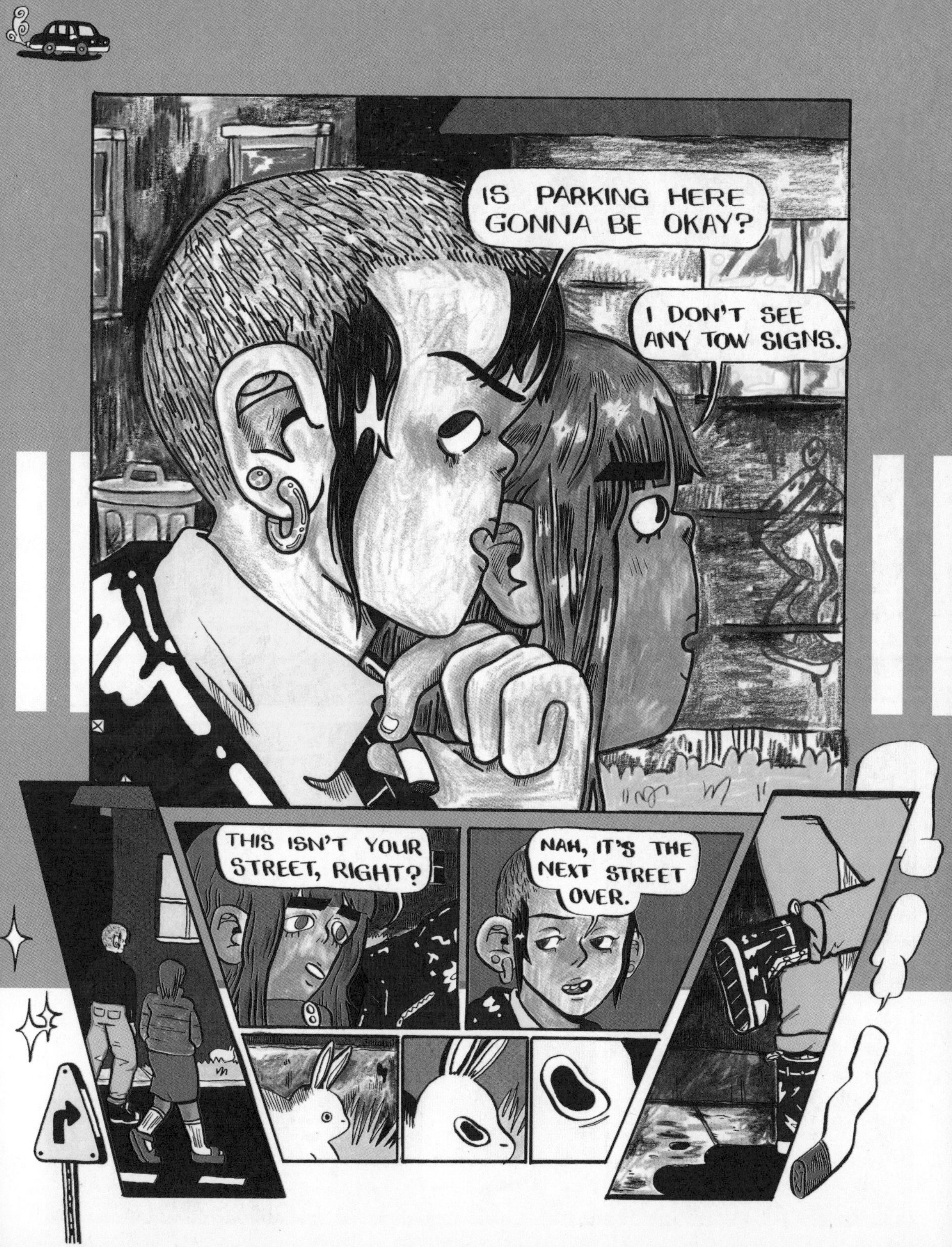
IS PARKING HERE GONNA BE OKAY?
I DON'T SEE ANY TOW SIGNS.
THIS ISN'T YOUR STREET, RIGHT?
NAH, IT'S THE NEXT STREET OVER.

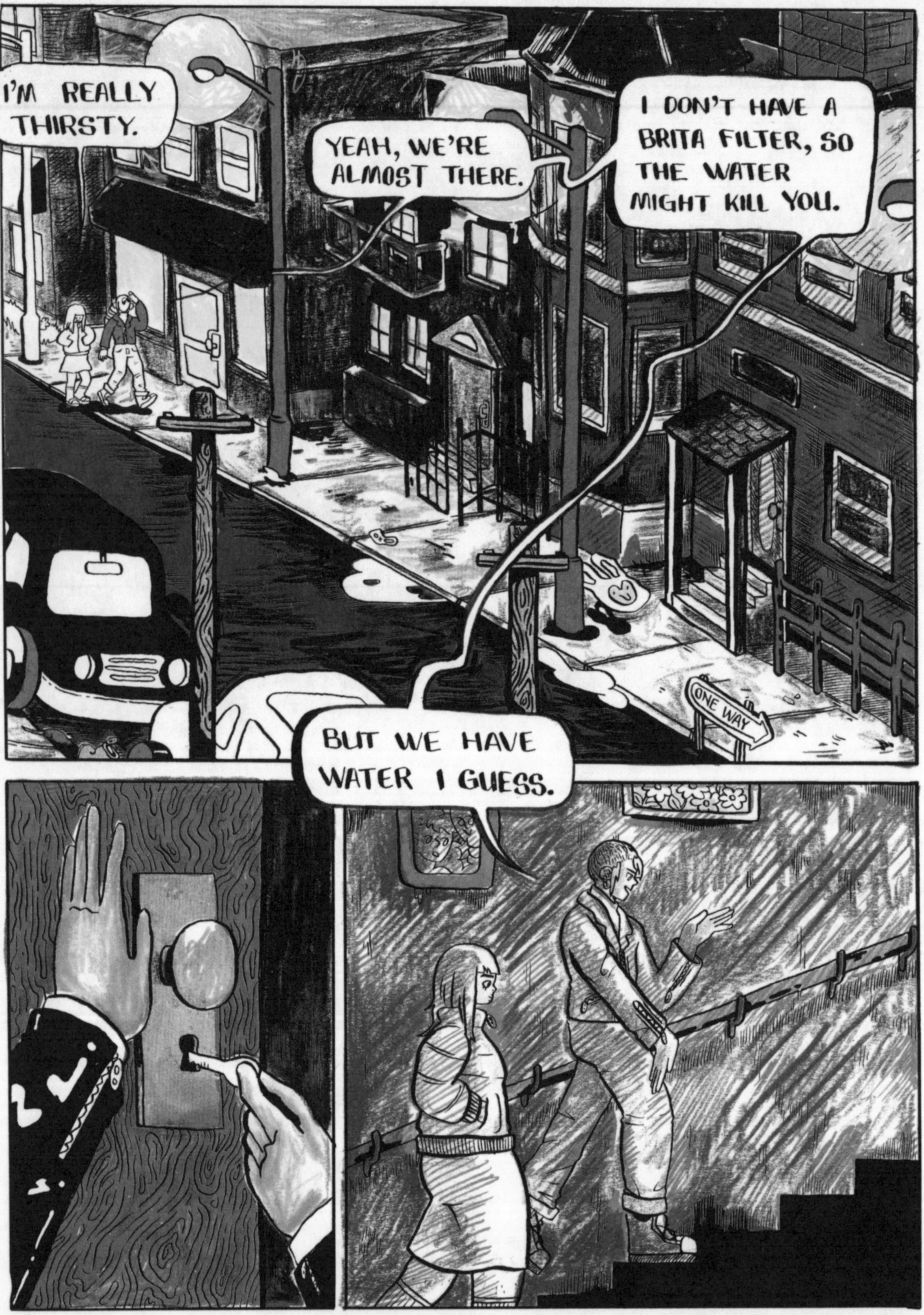
I'M REALLY THIRSTY.
YEAH, WE'RE ALMOST THERE.
I DON'T HAVE A BRITA FILTER, SO THE WATER MIGHT KILL YOU.
BUT WE HAVE WATER I GUESS.
ONE WAY

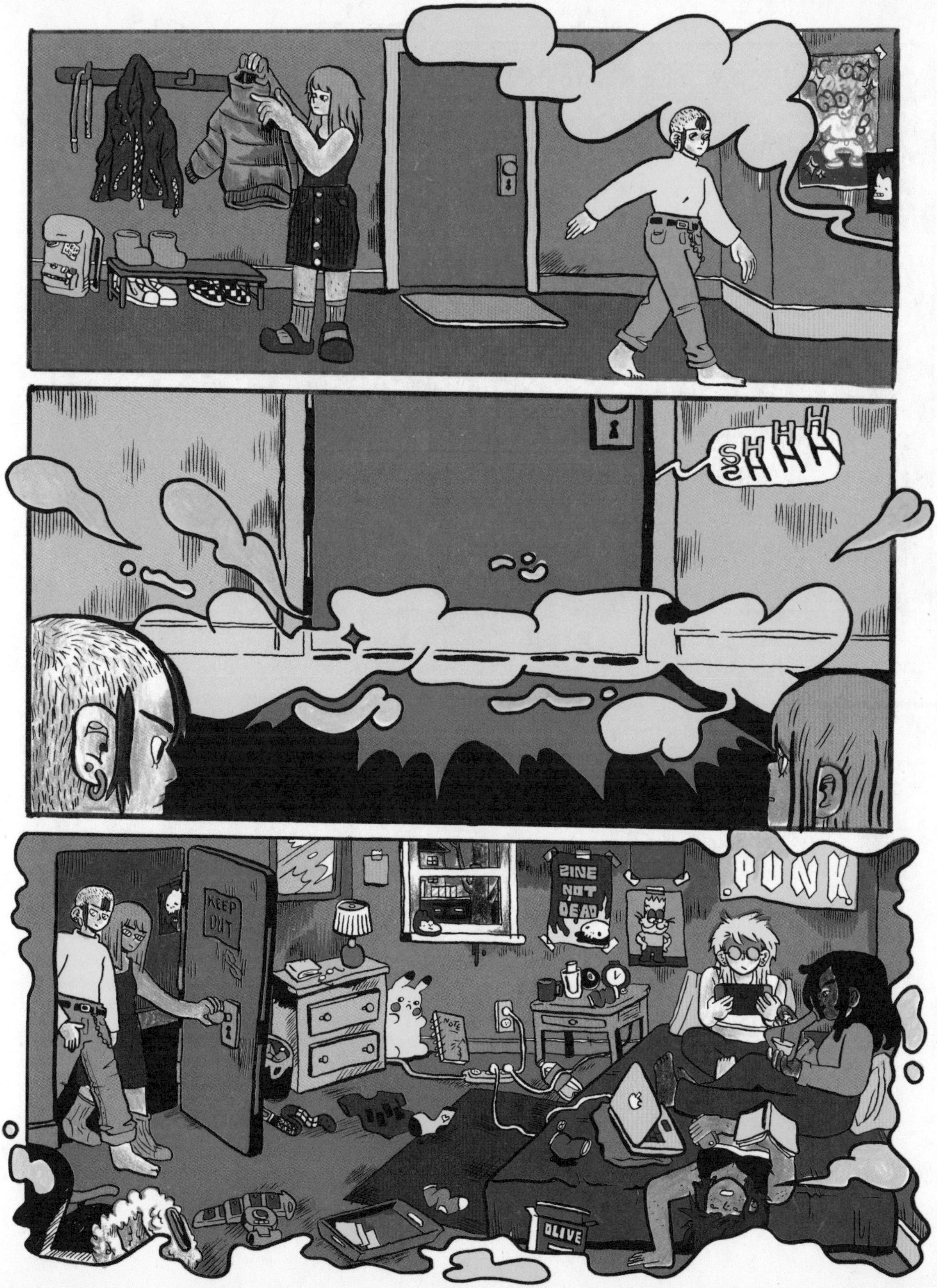
SHHH
KEEP OUT
ZINE NOT DEAD
PUNK
NOTE
OLIVE

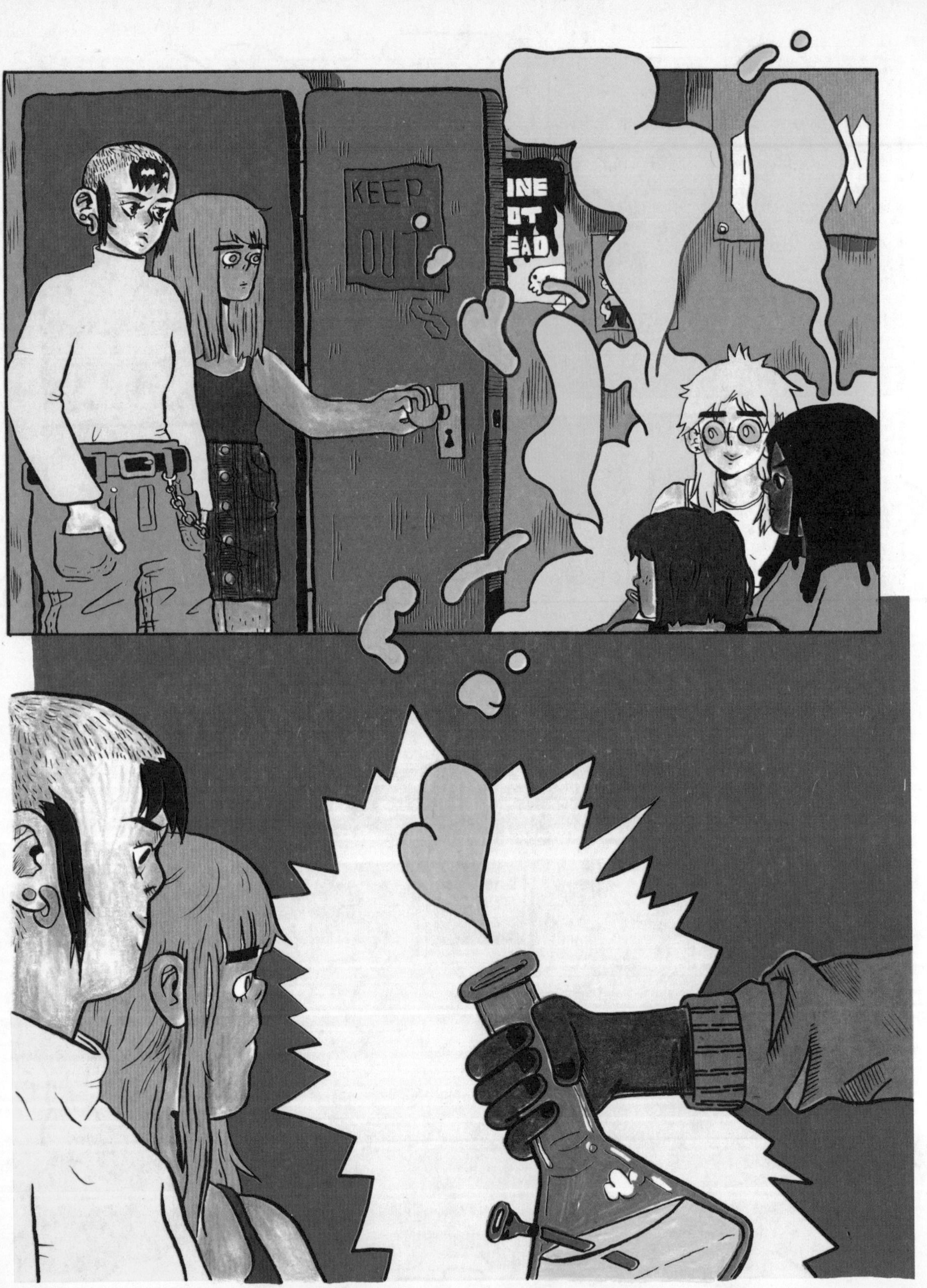
KEEP OUT

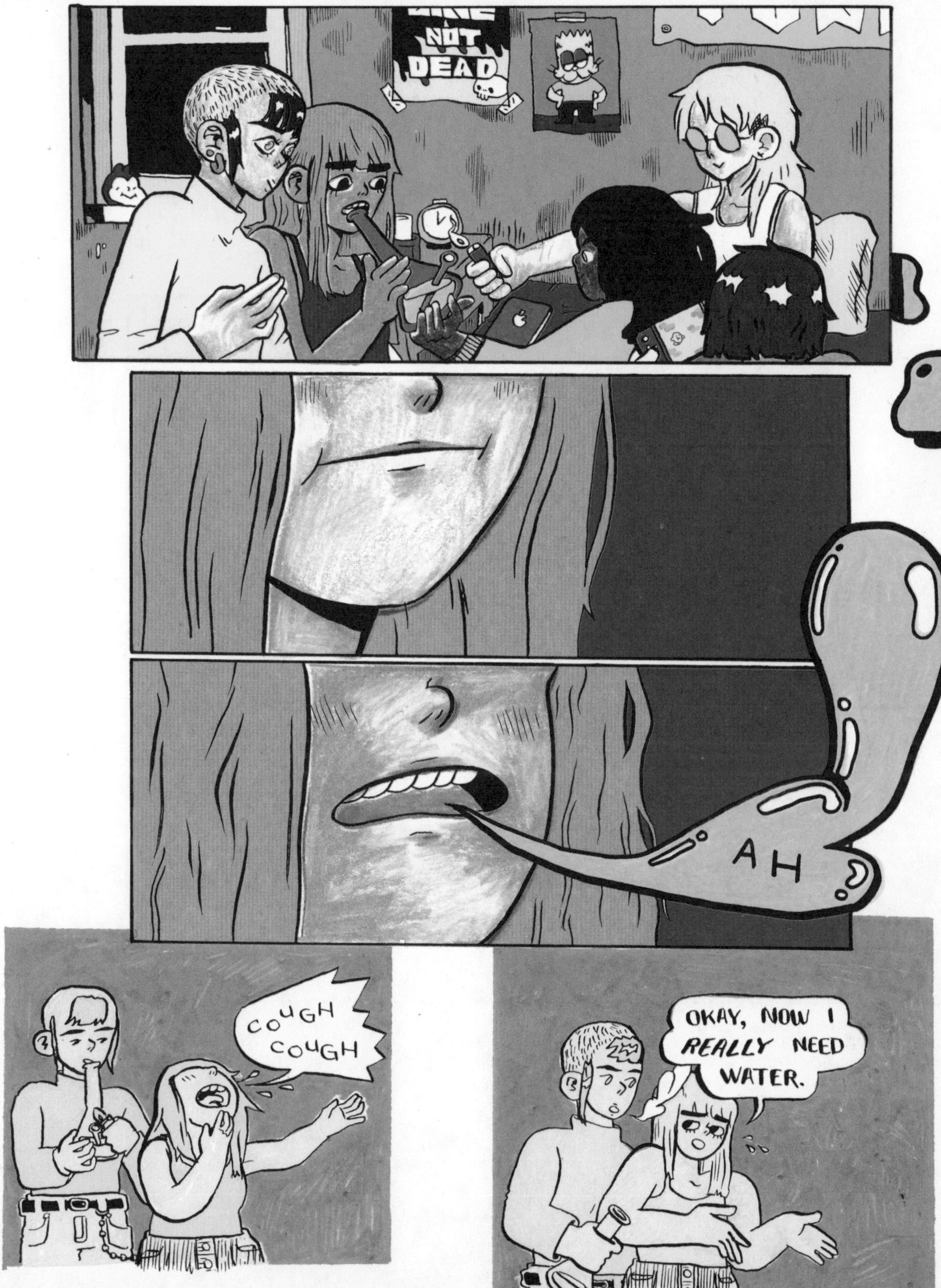
NOT DEAD
AH
COUGH COUGH
OKAY, NOW I REALLY NEED WATER.

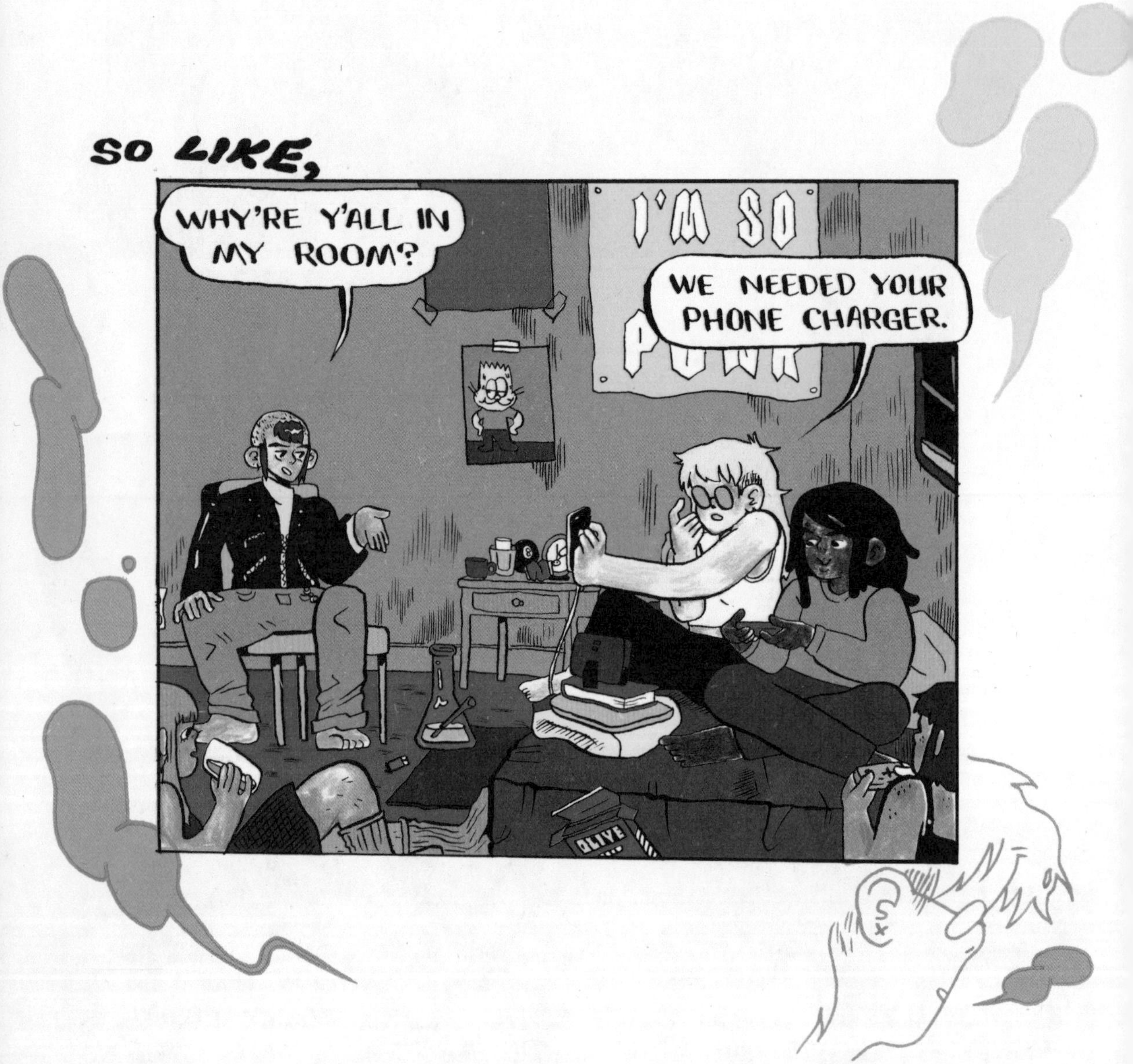
SO LIKE,
WHY'RE Y'ALL IN MY ROOM?
I'M SO
WE NEEDED YOUR PHONE CHARGER.
OLIVE

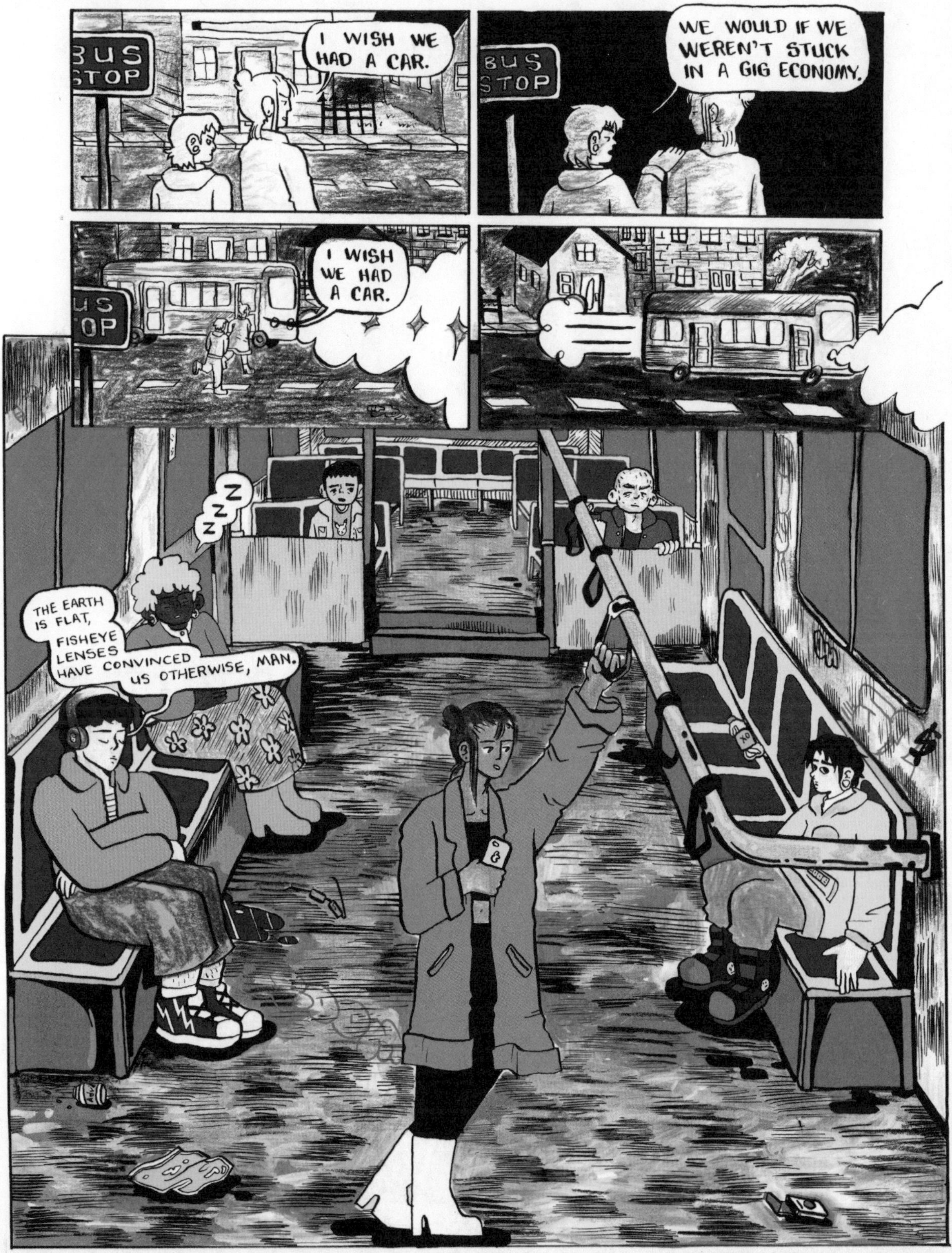

BUS STOP
I WISH WE HAD A CAR.
BUS STOP
WE WOULD IF WE WEREN'T STUCK IN A GIG ECONOMY.
BUS STOP
I WISH WE HAD A CAR.
Z Z Z
THE EARTH IS FLAT, FISHEYE LENSES HAVE CONVINCED US OTHERWISE, MAN.

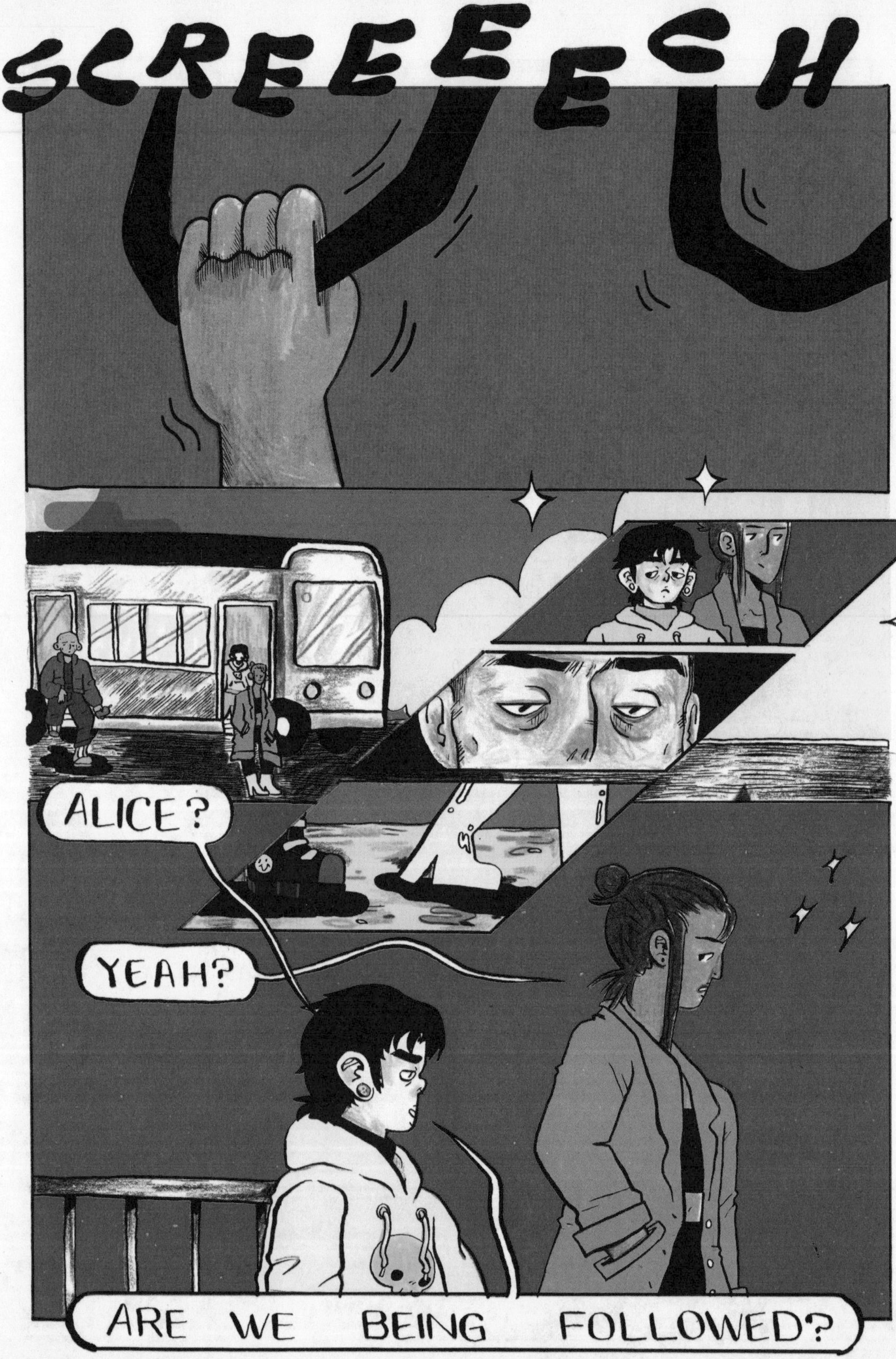
SCREEEECH
ALICE?
YEAH?
ARE WE BEING FOLLOWED?

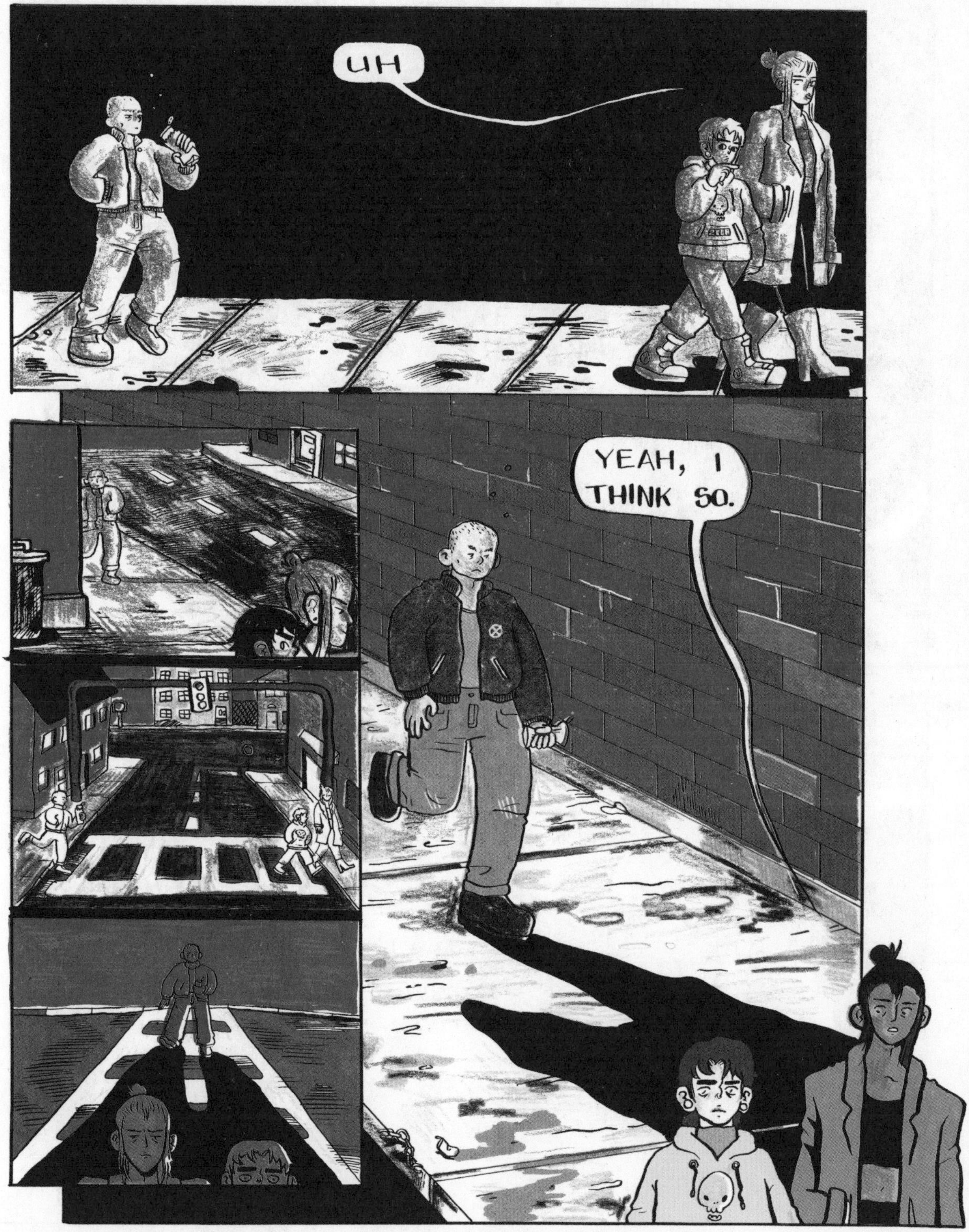
UH
YEAH, I THINK SO.

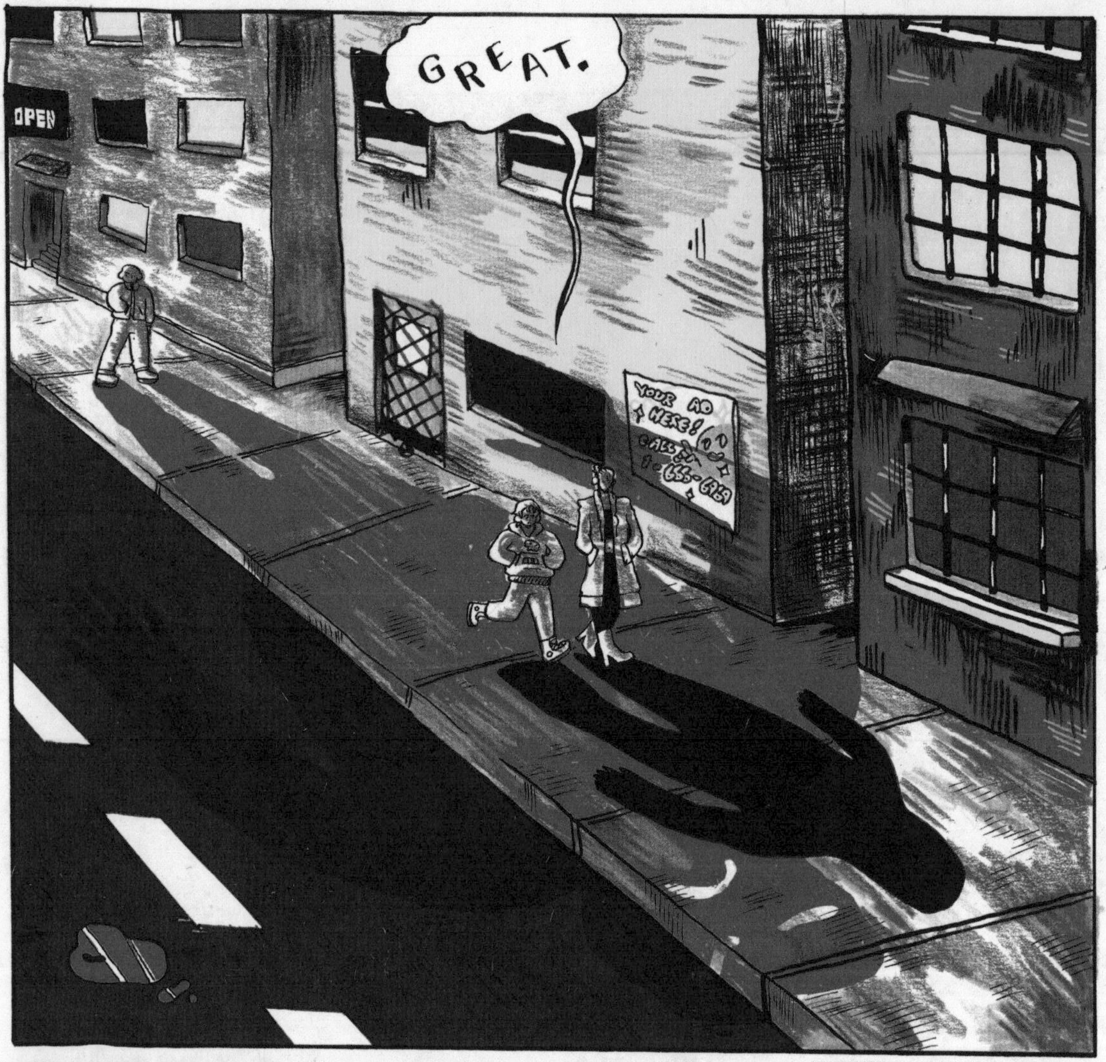
OPEN
GREAT.
YOUR AD HERE!
CALL
1-655-6969

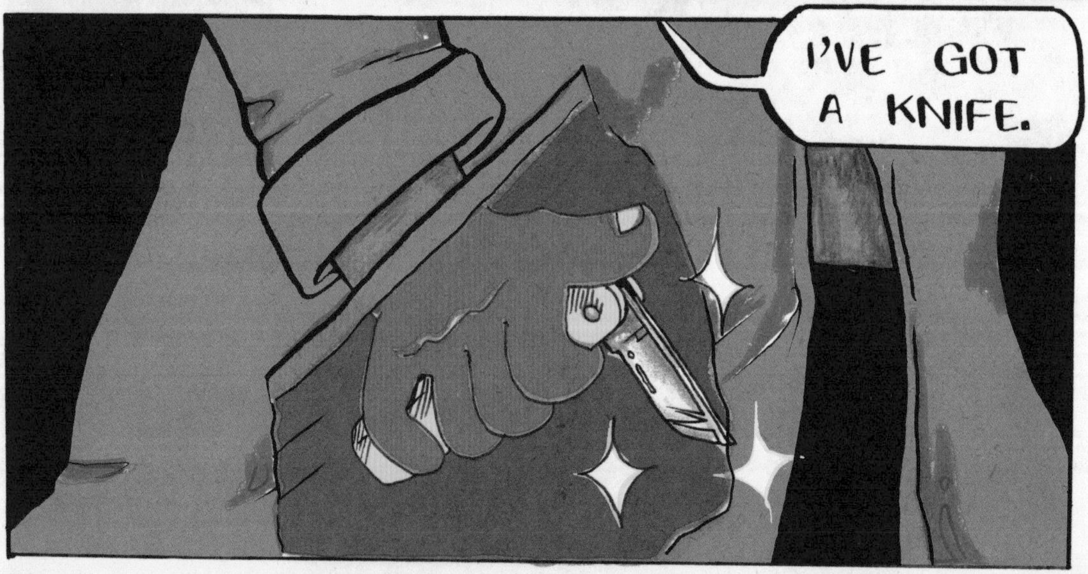
I'VE GOT A KNIFE.

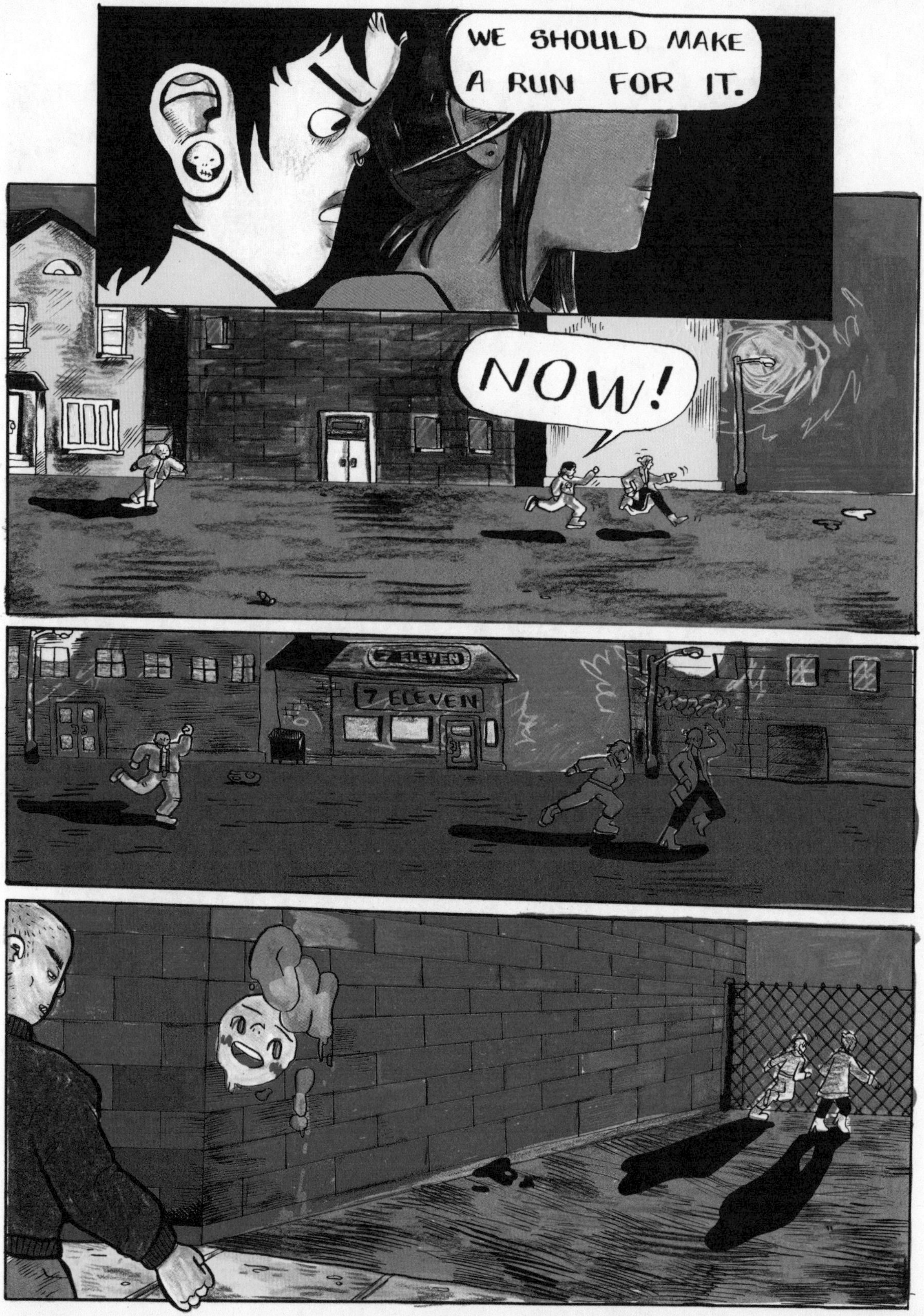
WE SHOULD MAKE A RUN FOR IT.
NOW!
7 ELEVEN
7 ELEVEN

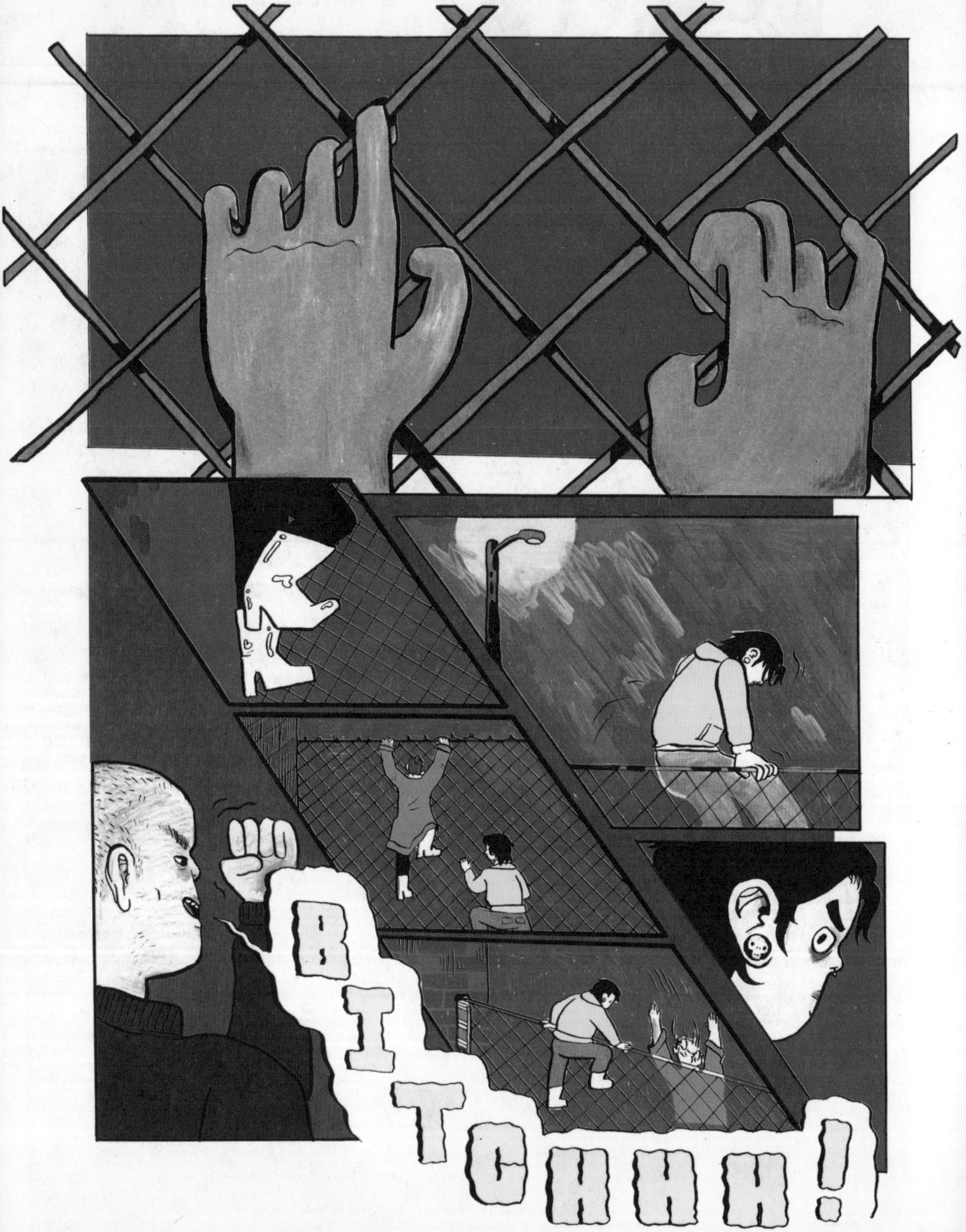
BITCHHH!

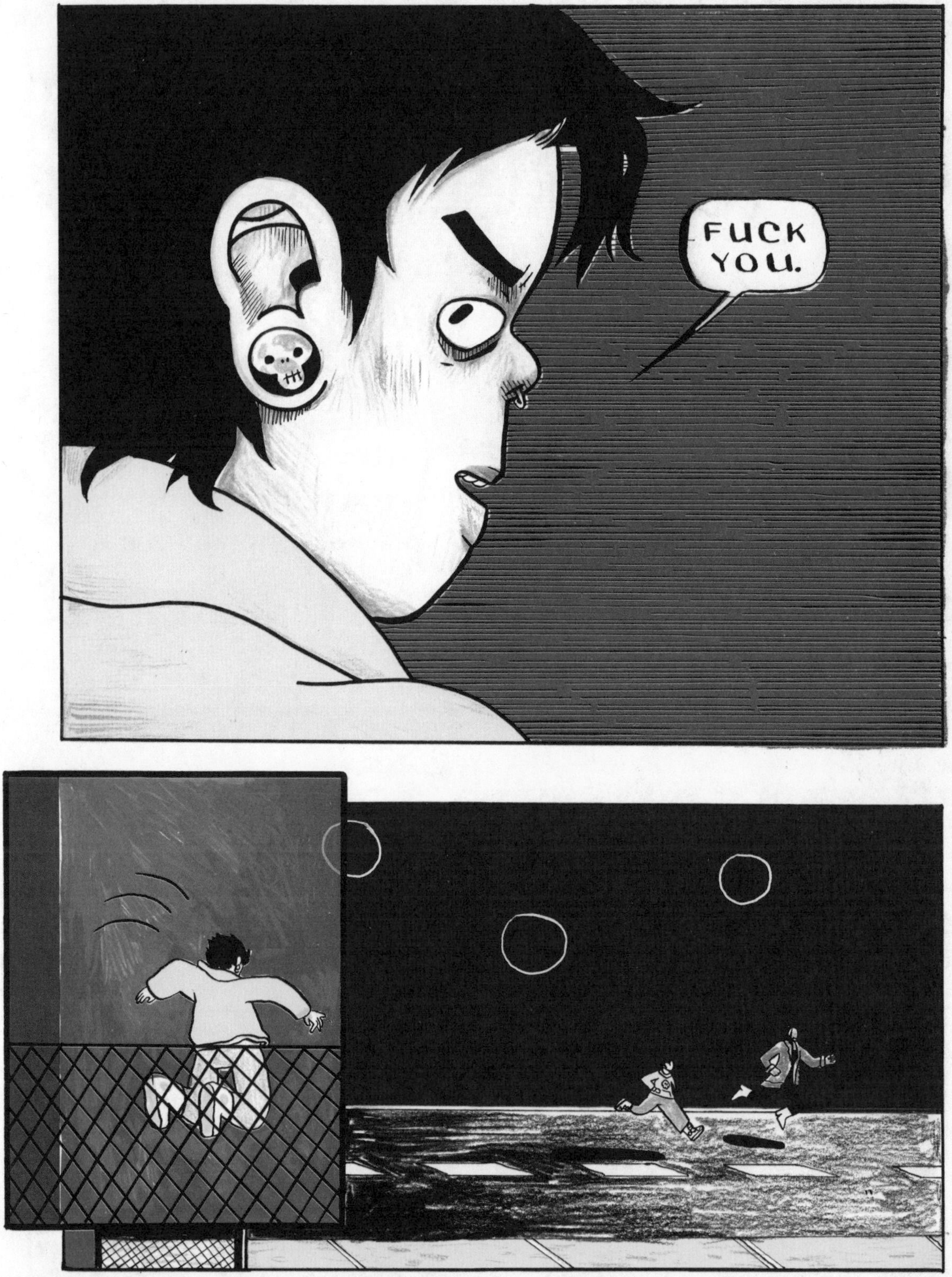
FUCK YOU.

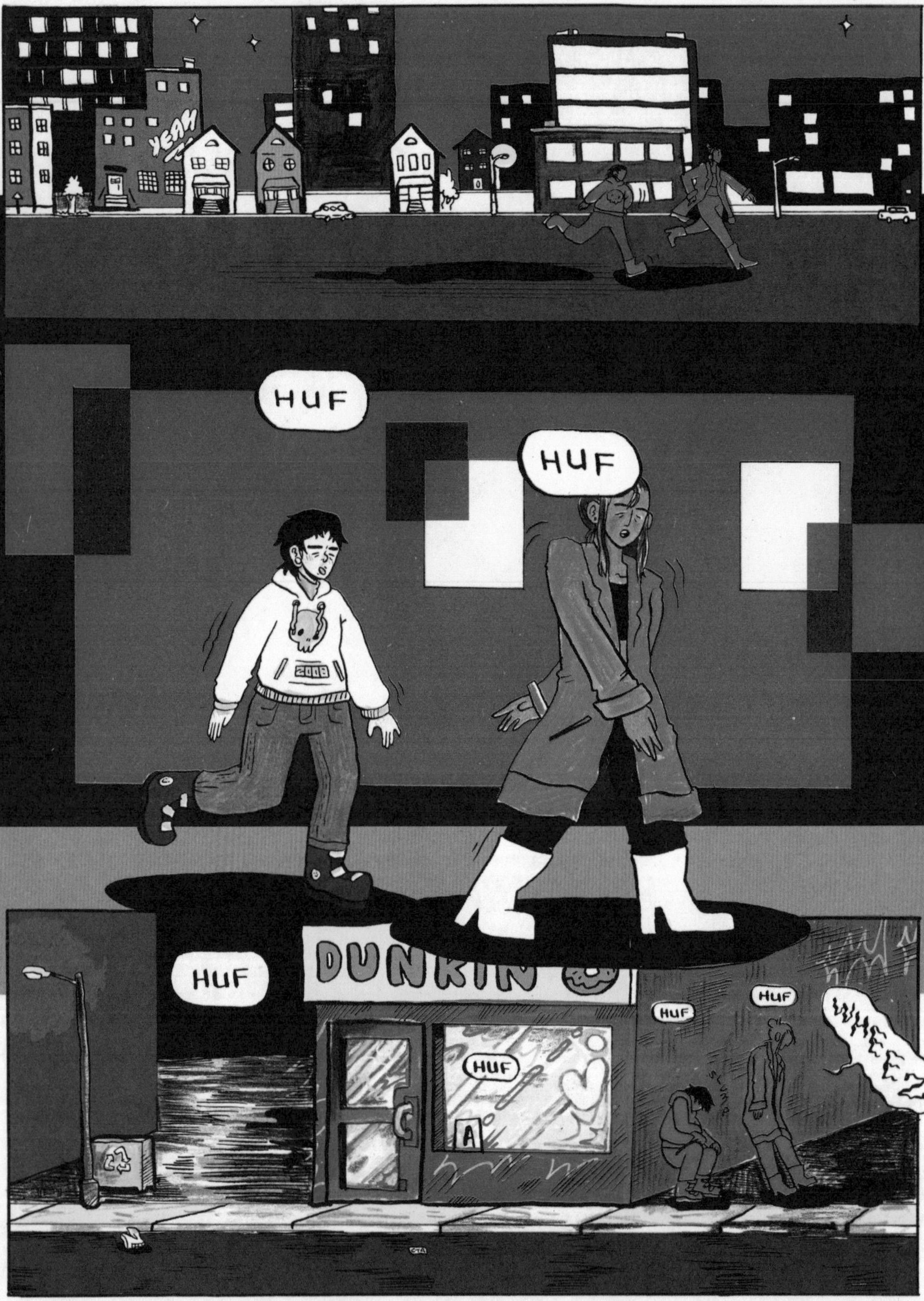
HUF
HUF
2008
HUF
DUNKIN
HUF
HUF
HUF
WHEEZ

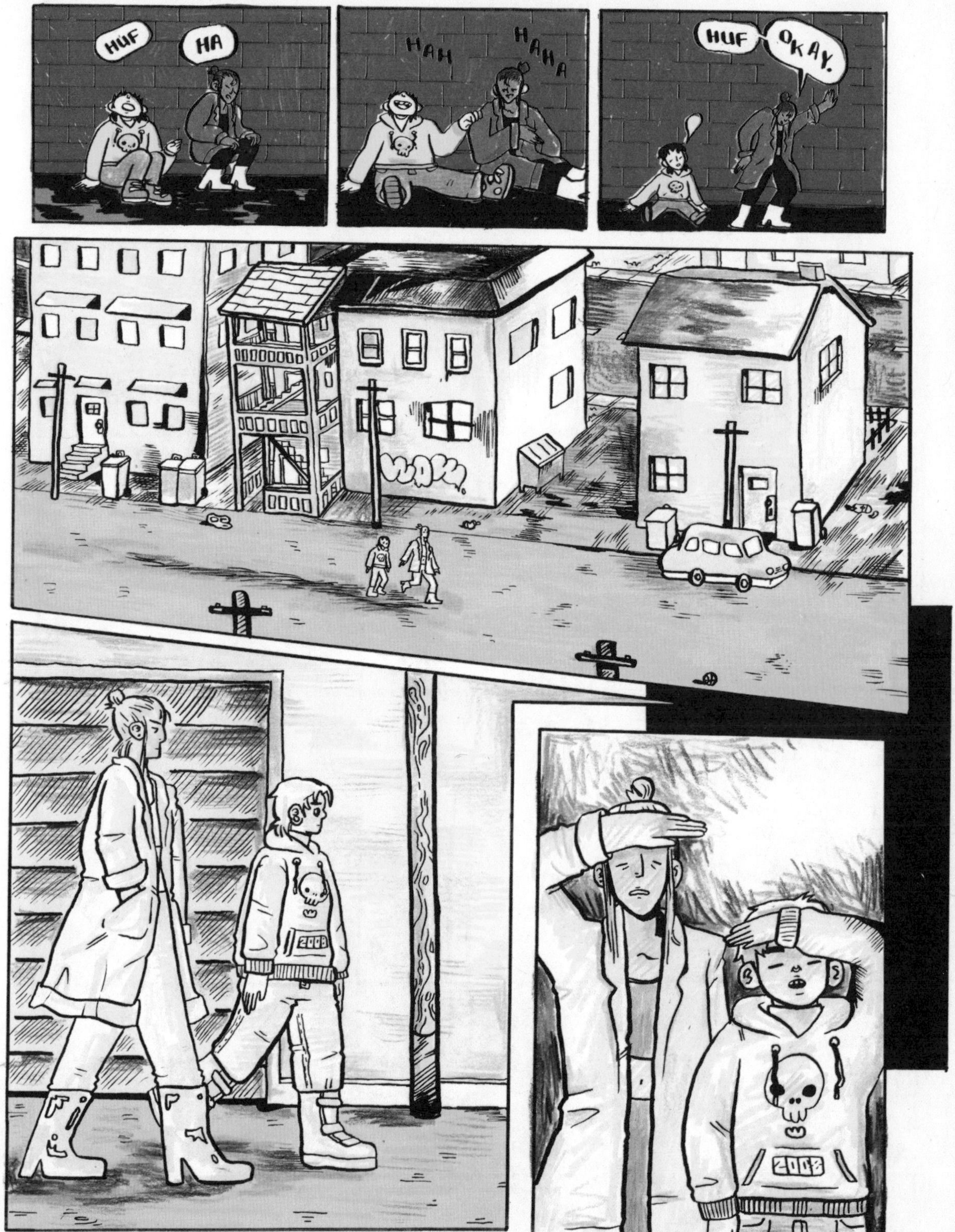
HUF
HA
HAH
HAHA
HUF
OKAY.

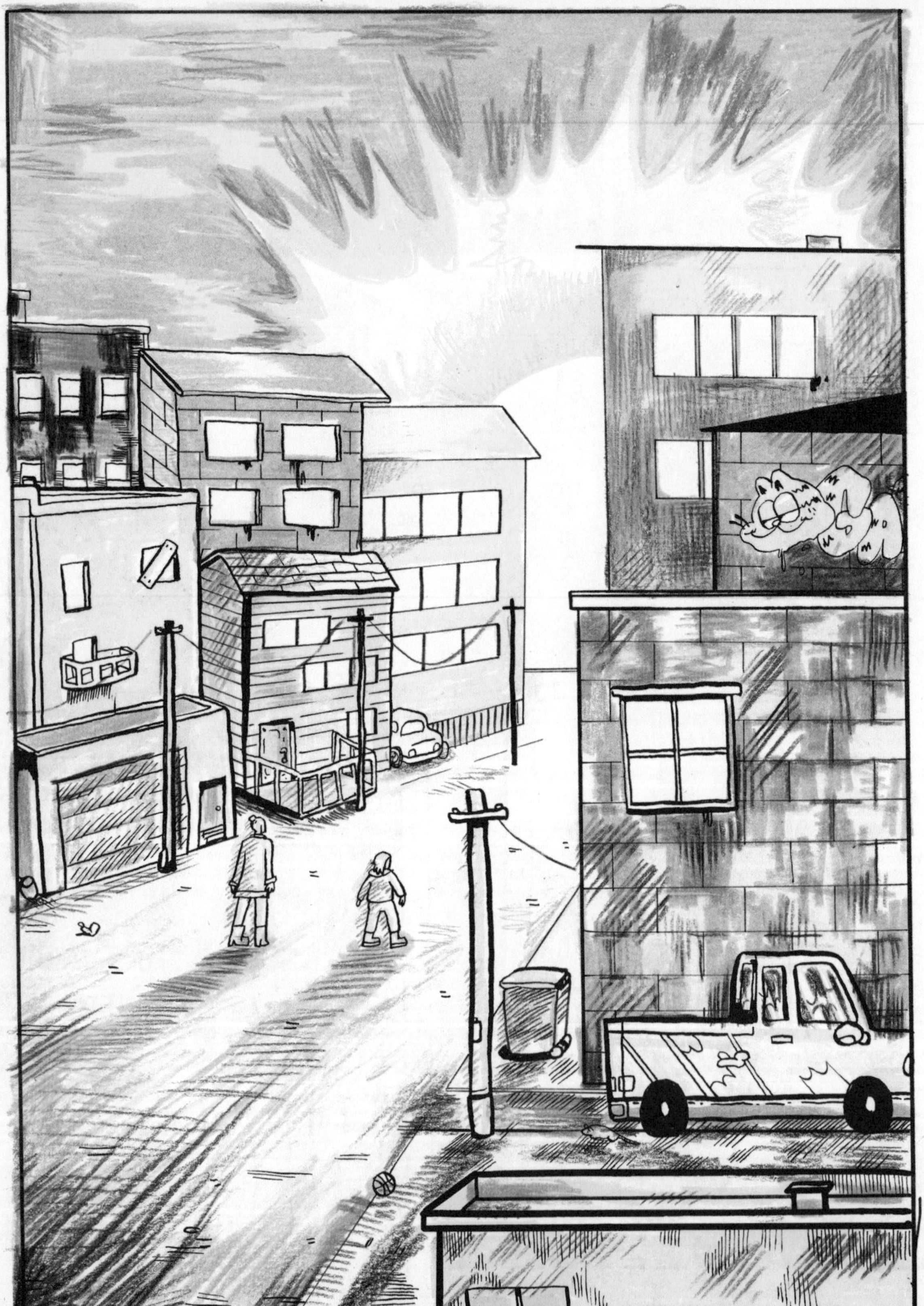

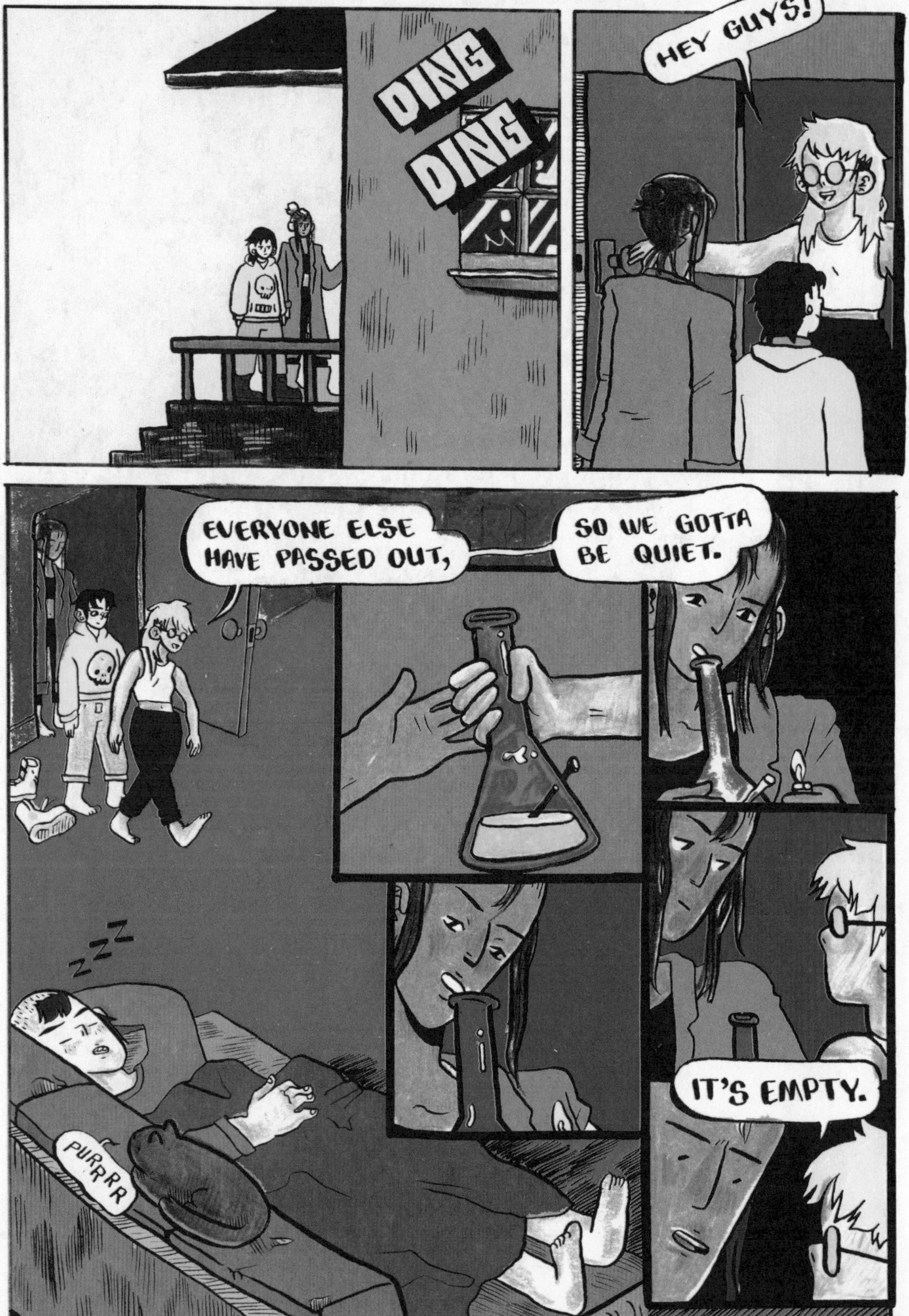
DING
DING
HEY GUYS!
EVERYONE ELSE HAVE PASSED OUT,
SO WE GOTTA BE QUIET.
ZZZ
PURRRR
IT'S EMPTY.

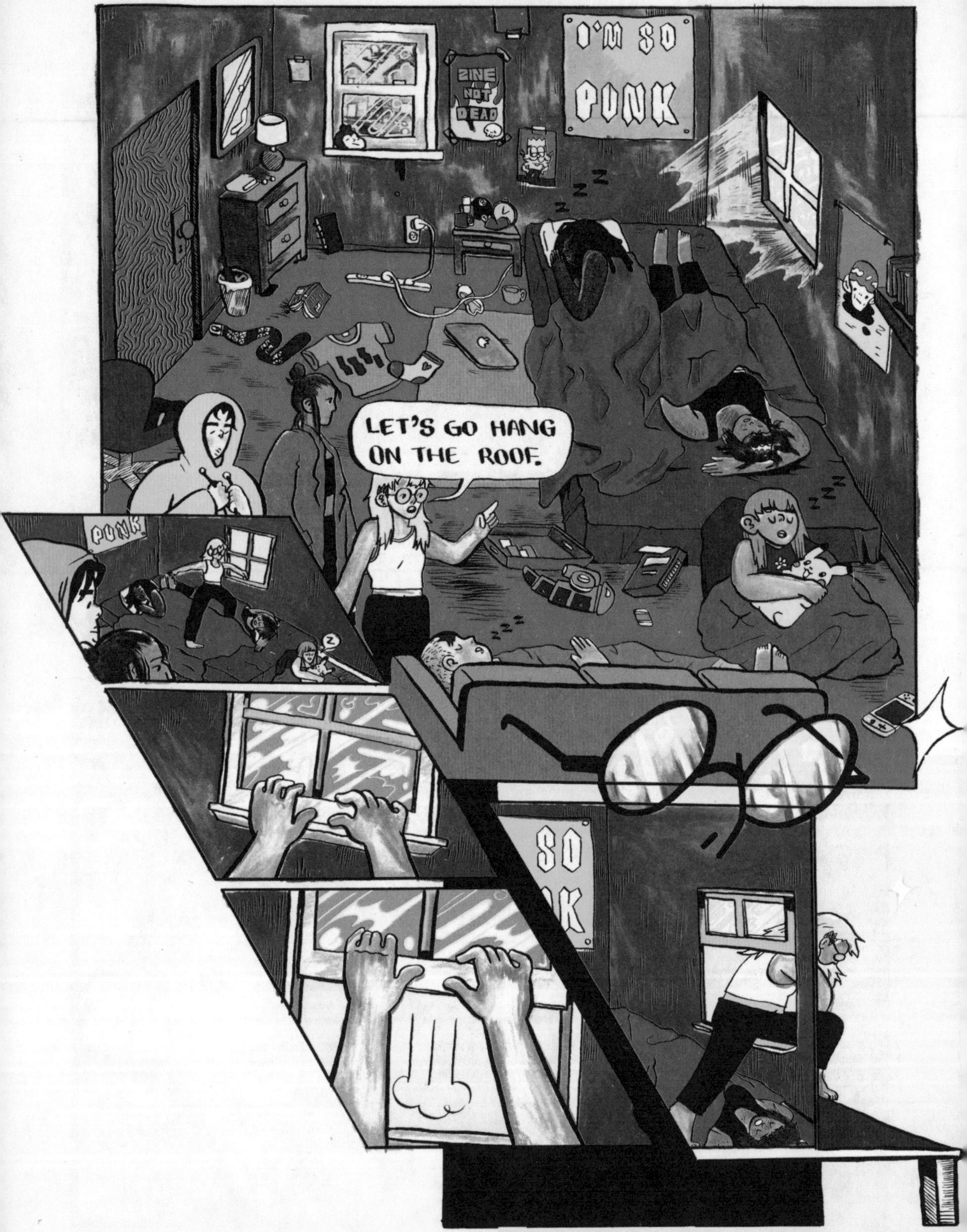
I'M SO PUNK
ZINE NOT DEAD
LET'S GO HANG ON THE ROOF.
PUNK
SO
OK

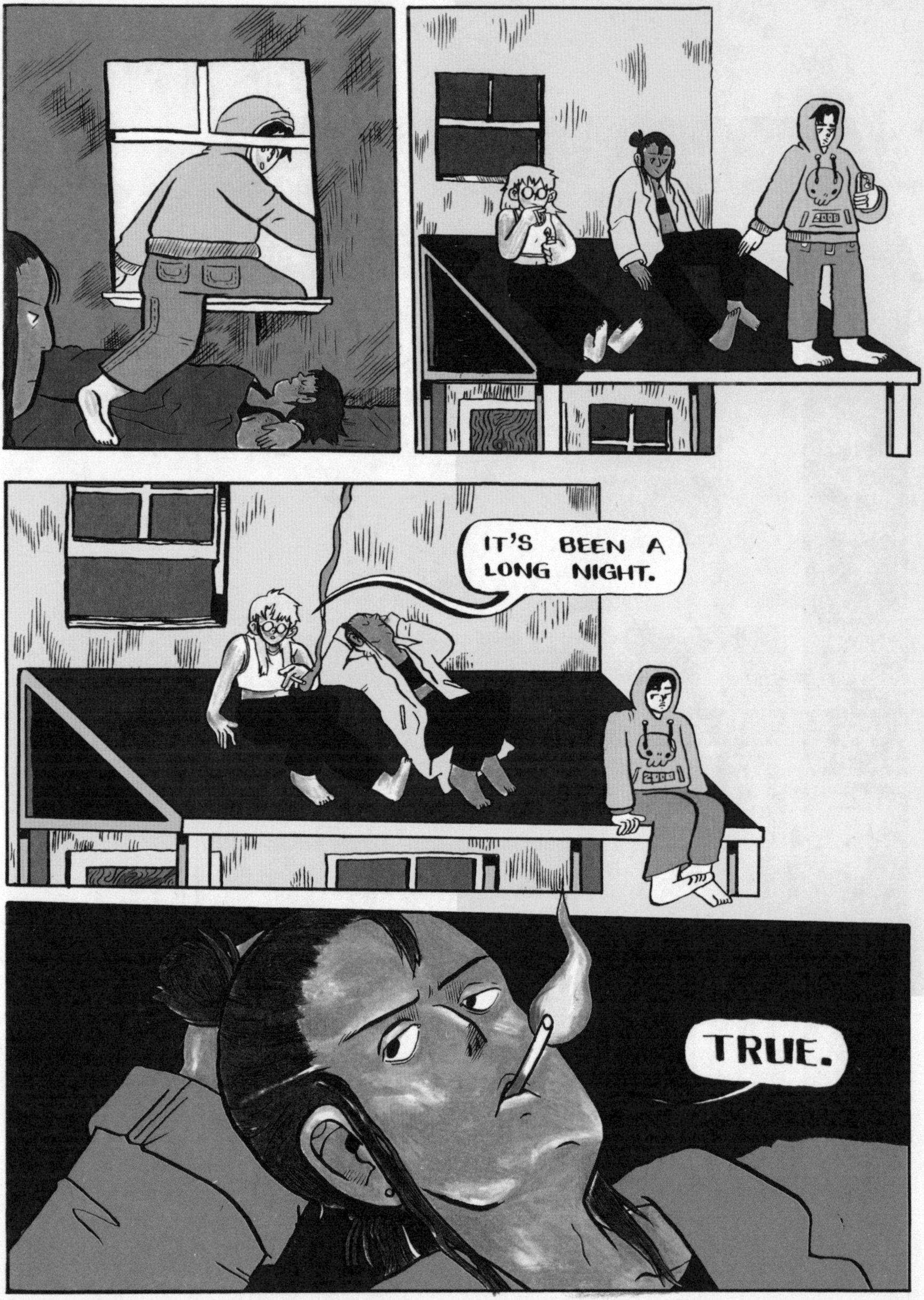
2008
2008
IT'S BEEN A LONG NIGHT.
TRUE.

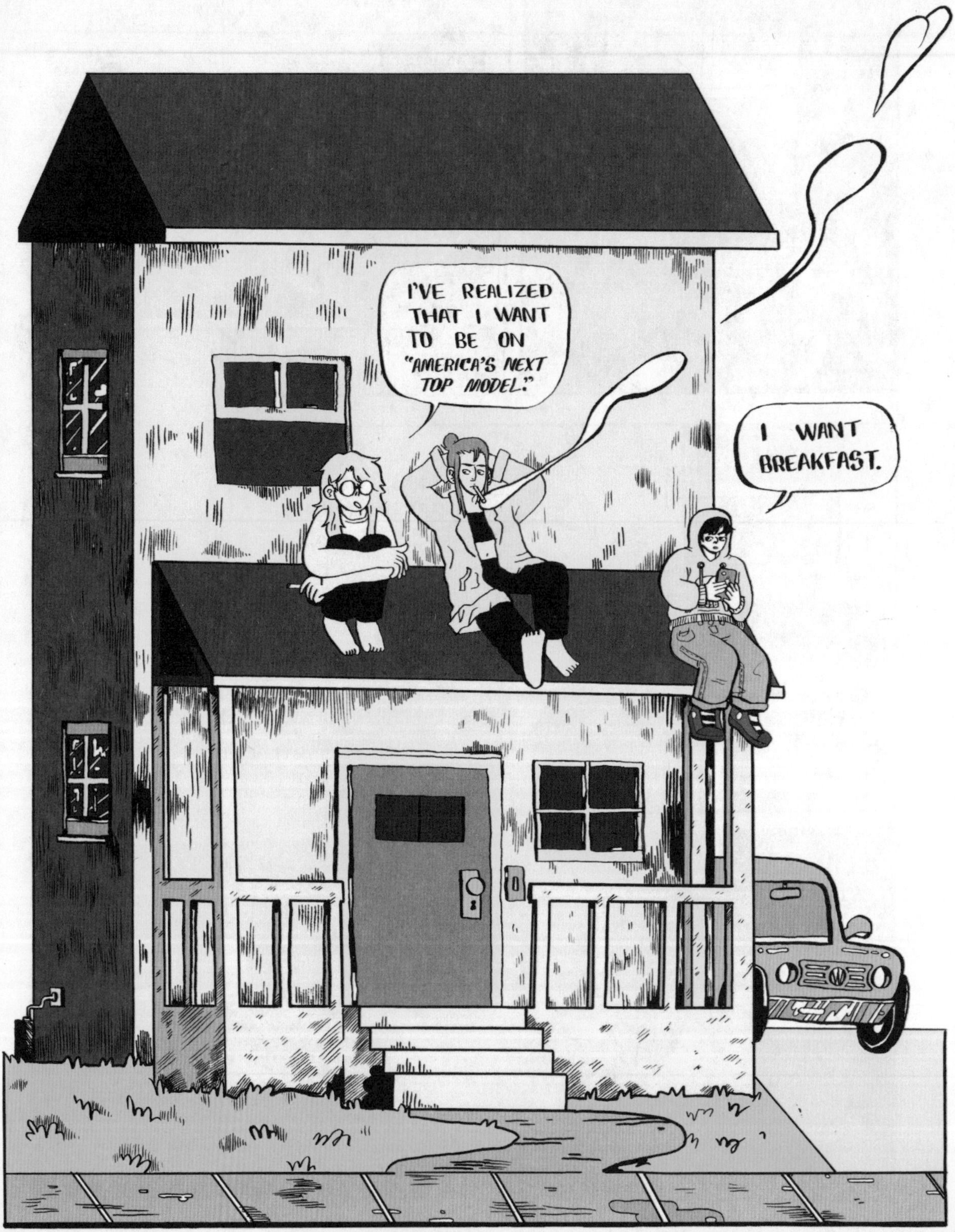
I'VE REALIZED THAT I WANT TO BE ON "AMERICA'S NEXT TOP MODEL."
I WANT BREAKFAST.

NO IDEA WHAT WILL END UP ON THE BACK OF THIS BOOK
DOES THIS COMIC EVEN PASS THE BECHDEL TEST?

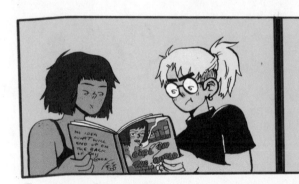

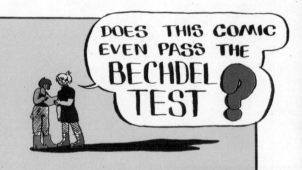

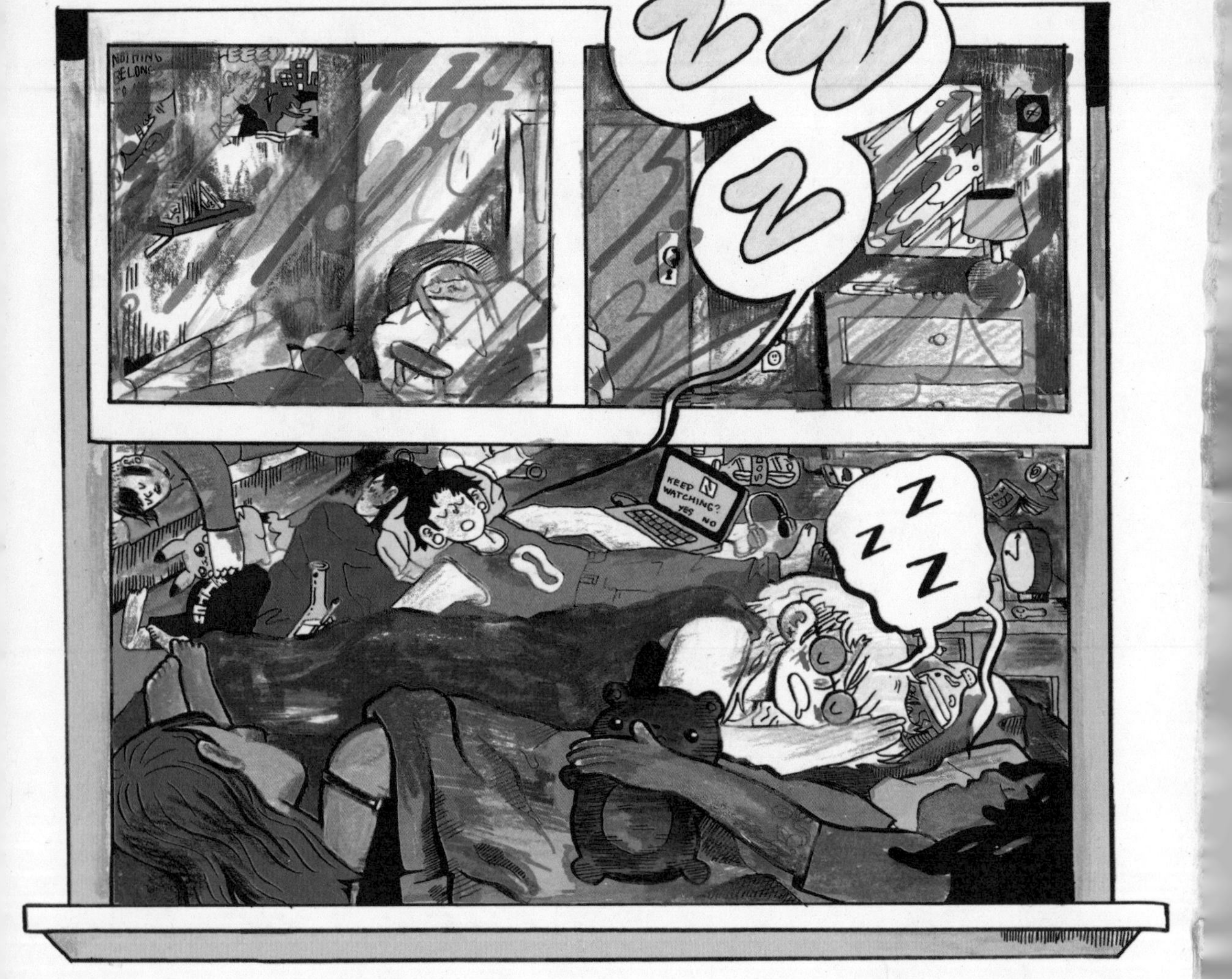
ZZZ
KEEP WATCHING? YES NO
ZZZ

SPECIAL THANKS TO:
AVI, CARINA, JESSICA, GABI,
MASON, JOE, NATALIE, HALLE,
PEI, MAC, DAN, DENA, TODD, PAUL,
AND MY MOM